P9-CFL-082

Perfect Phrases for Managers and Supervisors

Meryl Runion

McGraw-Hill
New York Chicago San Francisco Lisbon
London Madrid Mexico City Milan New Delhi
San Juan Seoul Singapore Sydney Toronto

ISBN 0-07-145216-8

Editorial and production services provided by CWL Publishing Enterprises, Inc., Madison, WI, www.cwlpub.com.

This publication is designed to provide accurate and authoritative information in regard to the subject matter covered. It is sold with the understanding that neither the author nor the publisher is engaged in rendering legal, accounting, or other professional services. If legal advice or other expert assistance is required, the services of a competent professional person should be sought.

> —*From a Declaration of Principles jointly adopted by a Committee of the American Bar Association and a Committee of Publishers*

McGraw-Hill books are available at special quantity discounts to use as premiums and sales promotions, or for use in corporate training programs. For more information, please write to the Director of Special Sales, Professional Publishing, McGraw-Hill, Two Penn Plaza, New York, NY 10121-2298. Or contact your local bookstore.

Contents

Contents

Contents

Contents

Contents

Contents

Contents

x

Introduction: How Perfect Phrases Help You Manage More Effectively

The Challenge of the Accidental Manager

A Harris poll concludes that up to 85% of people in management positions have never had management training. My informal surveys at management seminars tell me this figure is conservative. People are promoted into management positions daily … and often are expected to manage without training or guidance. They make it up as they go along, through trial and error, without any understanding of what is required to get results from others.

The situation is made even more challenging by the fact that the workplace is more diverse than ever. There are a wide variety of cultures and personalities and there is a new generation of workers entering the workforce that is different from any before it. For this generation, respect is not given automatically: it needs to be earned. This generation is outspoken and can be difficult to manage, … but not impossible. Management skills are more important than ever.

Those essential management skills need to be developed in a manager's "free time." The term "free time" gets laughter when

I use it in management seminars. The responsibility of management is often added to a work load that requires the new manager to do more with less. This leaves little or no time for new managers to study the skills necessary for success.

This book gives accidental (and intentional) managers and supervisors immediate benefits by providing words to use in hundreds of management situations. It is an essential reference that will allow you to manage more effectively by providing Perfect Phrases for almost every situation you are likely to face. They are quick and easy—and they work.

Why Perfect Phrases? The Importance of Planning Your Words

Perfect Phrases is another name for "PowerPhrases," a communication style I have been speaking and writing about for years. I have learned from years of management training and teaching PowerPhrases that if people do not know the words to say in a situation, they will usually not say anything at all. I frequently receive letters from managers who subscribe to my newsletter who tolerate inappropriate behavior from their subordinates. They ask me for the words to speak in situations they should have addressed years ago. When they find the words, they become willing to take action.

Other managers use aggressive words that create resistance, shut down communication, and backfire. Employees may respond to aggression in the short term, but it does not lead to maximum productivity and can cause passive-aggressive responses.

I have learned from teaching PowerPhrases around the world that most people alternate between passive and aggressive communication in sensitive situations. Most people do not know how to stay assertive—clear, direct, and respectful. Passive communication is ineffective. Aggressive communication creates resistance. Assertive communication gets results. Perfect Phrases are assertive phrases. They are valuable for managers to discover what effective, assertive wording is.

The Value of Scripting

Unless you are a management communication natural, it is valuable to plan your words in advance. Whenever a situation is challenging, tension tends to create a fight-or-flight style of thinking that produces a passive-aggressive mindset. It is difficult to think of options when you are triggered, but it is easier to recall phrases you planned in advance.

Many people resist using scripted phrases for fear of sounding phony. If this manner of speaking is not natural to you, you may sound unnatural at first. However, a "phony" assertive is more effective than a "genuine" passive or aggressive. Also, often the phrases are so appropriate that they can seem natural. These are the phrases you would choose yourself if only you had thought of them.

Perfect Phrases work. They communicate the goals of the organization and create a climate of clarity and trust. Clarity and trust are essential between you as a manager and the people you supervise. They help you hold your people accountable without blame. Language can be your most valuable management tool. Employees need the motivation, inspiration, and clear direction of Perfect Phrases.

How to Use This Book

One purpose of this book is for you to outgrow it. Here's how. This book is designed as a quick reference for every situation you face. Review relevant sections before you communicate. Adapt the phrases to your need and personal style. Repeat your phrases several times before you speak. After the conversation, review what you said and determine how you could have spoken more effectively.

If you are looking for a practical crash management course, read *Perfect Phrases for Managers and Supervisors* from cover to cover. As you discover the Perfect Phrases, you will not only learn powerful phrases, you will also learn what to do. This book gives you an overview of your management responsibilities and how Perfect PowerPhrases work for each of them.

If you have been managing for years, use this book as a review to make sure you are communicating effectively, as a tool to upgrade your skills, and as a reference to help you in specific situations. Turn directly to the chapter that covers your current issue. If your specific issue is not covered in this book, please e-mail us at info@speakstrong.com or adapt phrases for a similar situation in the book to your own. If you have a favorite phrase that you find useful, please pass it on to us so I can share it with my newsletter subscribers (*A PowerPhrase a Week*, www.speak-strong.com).

—Meryl Runion
President, SpeakStrong, Inc.

Chapter 1
The Principles That Make
PowerPhrases Perfect Phrases

As previously mentioned, Perfect Phrases is another name for PowerPhrases, a communication style I developed over many years. PowerPhrases and Perfect Phrases in this book are perfect because they are based on the fundamental rules of responsible communication. The rules help you embody characteristics people most admire in leaders. In *The Leadership Challenge*, authors James M. Kouzes and Barry Z. Posner asked people, "What qualities do you most look for and admire in a leader, someone whose direction you would willingly follow?" The top four characteristics are honest, forward-looking, competent, and inspiring.

The rules of responsible communication are based on those leadership qualities. They provide you with a code to guide your communication. Commit to them as a basis for your management communication. Encourage everyone to use them. Post a copy in your conference room, office, lunchroom, and coffee station. Before you post them, be sure you practice them yourself. When managers post rules they do not follow themselves, it breeds contempt. (A PDF version is available at www.powerpotentials.com/RunionRules.pdf.)

The Rules of Responsible Communication

A summary version of the rules is listed below, followed by an elaboration.

1. **Stay Positive:** Emphasize outcome and solutions. Choose your words to elevate and empower your employees. Examine problems and hold your employees and yourself accountable, not to blame, but to find solutions.
2. **Be Civil:** Be courteous and respectful. Speak the truth without viciousness or attack.
3. **Use Candor:** Be straightforward, direct, and open.
4. **Speak Accurately and Honestly:** Speak with precision, exactness, and adherence to facts. Be balanced in your use of facts. Limit yourself to reasonable interpretation of facts in all claims. Observe contextual correctness. Be informative and substantive.
5. **Listen Accountably:** Listen more than you speak. Listen as though you will be tested on understanding their words.
6. **Maintain the Three Perspectives:** Maintain awareness of the following three perspectives: yours, theirs, and that of a neutral party.

The Rules of Responsible Communication in Full

Stay Positive: The Importance of Creating Safety and Vision

Research shows that the vast majority of employees are motivated by a positive focus and demoralized by negativity. Positivity creates safety and openness. Negativity activates defensiveness and the fight-or-flight response. Managers who stay as positive as possible create safety, which is necessary to explore solutions. When your employee knows that his or her words will be received with good will, he or she feels free to be honest. If employees are fearful of attack, they are likely to censor their words or become defensive and attacking.

By maintaining a positive vision for the outcome throughout a conversation, you elevate all involved to their highest possible brain functioning. "Possibility thinking" inspires everyone, and ideas flow from a state of inspiration. This does not mean that problems are ignored. However, they are addressed in the light of possibility, which affects the entire tone and outcome of every conversation.

Be Civil: The Importance of Respect

Civility is essential to create safety in communication and to avoid triggering a fight-or-flight reaction. There are many common alienating language practices that disparage the listener, either intentionally or unintentionally. Civility does not mean denying or avoiding difficult realities. It means to be respectful, even if at the moment you do not believe that the other person deserves respect. To be civil, avoid the following:

1. **Sarcasm** that makes the person at whom it is directed the target of ridicule. (For example, "Did you do this all by yourself?" and "Yeah, like that's going to work!")
2. **Labeling and name-calling** that stereotypes others and puts them into a limited box. (For example, "You're not a team player" and "'Stubborn' over here doesn't like the idea.")
3. **Blame,** which condemns. The distinction between *blame* and *accountability* is difficult to discern. Accountability

seeks to understand. Blame attacks. Employees must be held accountable. Blame is not necessary and is often unproductive. (For example, "This is your fault" vs. "I see some things you could have done to avoid this. Let's look at what they are so this won't happen again.")

4. **Emotional manipulation**, which attempts to place emotional pressure on others. This includes attempts to make someone feel guilty, to shame someone into compliance, to deliberately trigger anger, or to manipulate fears. (For example, "If you respected me, you would have…" and "After all I've done for you….") Any type of emotional manipulation is improper and irresponsible.

5. **Absolute language** that oversimplifies the truth and limits understanding to simplistic, black-and-white concepts. ("You are with us or you are against us.") "Always" and "never" are examples of black-and-white language we want to avoid. ("You're always sarcastic.")

6. **Threats,** which use coercion to intimidate. They are an attempt to force someone into doing what you want. There is a subtle but important distinction between threatening someone and informing someone of the consequence of his or her action. Threats are intended to force others to choose the path you want them to take. Informing of consequences is intended to tell someone about the choice you will make based on what he or she does, so his or her choice of action is informed. (For example, this statement is a threat: "If you value your job, you'll do as you're told." This statement informs of consequences: "This work is part of your job description and needs to be done. If you are not willing to do it, I'll have to replace you with someone who will.")

Use Candor: The Importance of Being Straightforward

One benefit of being straightforward, direct, and open is that it creates trust and confidence. Candor dispels the need to deduce meanings, probe for hidden implications, or risk being blindsided. Candor can be uncomfortable in the moment, but combined with civility it ultimately builds relationships. Part of PowerPhrases is to say what you mean and tell the truth about what you think, feel, and want.

Managers who keep secrets create cultures of distrust. When employees know they can count on their manager to keep them abreast of things that affect them, it creates confidence. When they do not trust their managers, it creates uncertainty and causes employees to speculate. Often the imagined reality is far worse than the actual reality.

Speak Accurately and Honestly: The Importance of Credibility

Distortion is a violation of the communication rules, even if the words spoken are literally true. There are many ways to distort the truth. Statistics can be manipulated, partial truths can mislead, and facts can be exaggerated. Sometimes these efforts are deliberate. Other times the speaker maintains the illusion in himself or herself that he or she is being truthful.

Responsible communication rejects all forms of deception. Accuracy is essential for effective communication. All parties need to be certain they can trust the veracity of what they hear. Speak with precision, exactness, and adherence to facts by observing the following guidelines:

1. **Balance your use of facts.** Choose facts that are representative of the whole and avoid the implication that the

exception is the rule. For example, if you have 13 complaints about a procedure and one person who likes it, it would be a distortion for you to speak of the one person who likes it and fail to mention the 13 complaints. While that is a literal truth, it still distorts the truth.

2. **Limit yourselves to reasonable interpretation of facts in all claims.** Interpret facts only in a way any reasonable person might. For example, it is not a reasonable interpretation of the facts to say that someone who questioned the efficacy of a procedure is disloyal. It is not a reasonable interpretation to suggest that someone who made a single mistake is irresponsible.

3. **Observe contextual correctness.** Information used out of context is inappropriate and violates trust. If you look for evidence to support any theory, you are likely to be able to find something, especially when used out of context. Accuracy and honesty require that quotes and examples be used to convey the same message they would when provided in context. For example, if someone says, "I'm not sure about what I'm doing," referring to using a new software program, it would not be contextually correct to tell his manager that you believe the person is incompetent in his job because he said he was not sure about what he was doing.

4. **Be informative and substantive.** While emotional appeals can be effective and emotional displays can get results, ultimately it is more productive to be insightful than "inciteful." Communicate to educate and add to the understanding of the listener. Make certain all claims have a solid basis of information that is researched and substantiated. For example, if

your company is being bought out, there will probably be talk about the job losses that will ensue. This can incite fear in employees. However, the responsible communicator will investigate the history of the acquiring company's former acquisitions and the stated plans before speaking and will include the basis for his or her opinions in any discussion.

Listen Accountably: The Importance of Knowing What They Think

Listening well pays off. It helps you understand the other person's position. It reduces defensiveness. It wins respect. It facilitates problem solving. When you listen, listen as though you were going to be tested on what they say. Listen for the three crucial points: what they think, what they feel, and what they want. Clarify your understanding of these points by saying something like this: "Let me be sure my understanding is correct. My understanding is that you think…, feel…, and want…. Is my understanding correct?" This ensures that your assumptions about what they are saying are accurate.

Maintain the Three Perspectives: The Importance of Standing in Everyone's Shoes

There are three perspectives to every conversation—yours, theirs, and the one a neutral party would tell. It is much easier to view the three perspectives when you are not personally involved, but as soon there is personal involvement, the blinders go on. Although difficult, it *is* possible to be aware of the three perspectives when you are personally involved. Have all parties ask these questions:

- What do I think, feel, and want?
- What do they think, feel, and want?

■ How would a neutral party describe this conversation/situation?

This technique helps you to stay aware of all three perspectives at all times.

PowerPhrases: The Perfect Phrases to Use for Responsible Communication

The rules of responsible communication are the principles to guide responsible communication. PowerPhrases are the tools to speak in accordance with those rules. The remainder of the book lists PowerPhrases—Perfect Phrases for hundreds of situations. This section tells you how to create your own.

PowerPhrases are short, specific, targeted expressions that say what you mean so you can mean what you say without being mean when you say it.

Short: Keep instructions, feedback, and all important communications brief to avoid confusing the issue or diluting your message.

Specific: Chose precise words that provide as much information as possible. For example, specify deadlines. Answer the questions: who, what, when, where, and how.

Targeted: Select your words for the results you seek. Have a goal in mind and consider the consequences for every statement you make.

Say what you mean: Communicate what you think, feel, and want. Be guided by the truth as you know it, rather than the response that is likely to be safe or popular.

The Principles That Make PowerPhrases Perfect Phrases

Mean what you say: Protect the integrity of your words by following through on what you say. Speak only words you are committed to follow up on.

Don't be mean when you say it: Be kind in your choice of words. Refrain from using the communication tactics detailed under the "Be Civil" guideline of the communication rules—sarcasm, labeling and name-calling, blame, emotional manipulation, absolute language, and threats.

There will be times when it will be tempting and/or convenient to ignore the principles of responsible communication. Don't do it! If you ignore the temptation and consistently use the rules, you will embody the qualities employees say they want in a leader: honest, forward-looking, competent, and inspiring. You will be a leader others follow, not by necessity, but by choice.

Let the Perfect Phrases begin!

Chapter 2
Put Your Best Foot Forward: Perfect Phrases to Establish Your New Role

It's not easy being new. Your employees are not sure about your authority and, many times, neither are you. A good beginning is essential. Set the tone the very first day.

Phrases for the beginning of your new role need to establish your authority without stepping on toes. Oftentimes you'll be supervising former peers. Sometimes you'll manage someone who wanted your position. Sometimes you will be tested. There are those who will attempt to take advantage of your status as a new manager. Perfect Phrases provide you with the tools to manage those situations.

As a new manager, use Perfect Phrases to address issues *before* they manifest.

Perfect Phrases to Address Former Peers Who Are Now Your Employees

- I will need your help, understanding, and support in my new role as your manager.

- Changing roles is difficult for all of us. It is important for us to talk openly about any bumps we find on the road.

- I know how much we used to complain about the boss before I became the boss. I want to give you the freedom to talk among yourselves about me. I also invite you to come to me directly when you have issues.

- I know employees have turned criticism of management into an art form. I invite you to practice that art form with me directly instead of among each other.

- I'm not comfortable criticizing upper management with you anymore. However, if you have an issue you need help with, I'm here for you.

Perfect Phrases to Address Friends Who Are Now Your Employees

- I value your friendship and that won't change. During business hours, I am a manager first. Please don't take it personally.

- It will be difficult for both of us if I am suspected of favoritism toward you. I will be careful to avoid that. Please don't take it personally, but also be sure to let me know if I take it too far.

- Outside of the office, I am your friend. Inside the office, I am your manager. I want to excel at both.

- This is an awkward situation because we are so close. How can I best give you direction and correction without damaging our friendship?

- How do you recommend I manage you so our personal friendship doesn't interfere with our work?

Perfect Phrases to Address Employees Who Wanted the Promotion You Got

- I know you wanted this position. This is a tough situation for us both. Can I count on you to support me the way you would have wanted me to support you?

- Do you want to talk about how you feel about me getting this promotion?

- If I hadn't gotten this promotion, I think I would have felt some resentment toward the person who did. Is it possible that you feel that way?

- If there is anything you want to talk about, I'm here.

- I understand your frustration and even anger. I think that's normal. How can I help us move past this and focus on our goals?

- This is awkward for both of us. How do you see us working together as a team?

Perfect Phrases to Address the Acting Supervisor You Are Replacing

- I need your help with the transition. Can I count on that?

- Tell me three things you do that work really well managing this team and three things to avoid.

- If people go to you instead of me, will you let me know? I know they're used to going to you, and I need to know what's going on.

- In the beginning you'll know more than I do, so it will make sense for people to go to you instead of me. Will you refer them to me anyway, so we can transition quickly and smoothly? Thanks!

Perfect Phrases to Set the Tone

- I want you to continue doing business as usual. I don't plan to make changes until I understand why things are done the way they are.

- I do not have preconceived notions about anyone or what changes, if any, need to be made.

- I will observe you in your job at times. This is as much for me to learn what you do as anything else. However, I may have a few questions or suggestions for you.

- I believe in teamwork and cooperation, and I will be expecting that from you as well.

- I will keep you informed on anything that affects you. I trust you will be open with me as well.

- I plan to meet with each of your privately to see how we can support each other.

Perfect Phrases for Your Initial Employee Meetings

Schedule a meeting with each of your new employees just to get to know them and address any issues before they become problems.

- What do you expect from me as your manager?
- Are there obstacles for you in doing your job that I might be able to help you with?
- What motivates you?
- What are some things managers have done in the past that have worked well for you?
- What are some things managers have done in the past that have not worked well for you?
- If you had advice for me as your new manager, what would it be?
- What is the biggest thing you'd like to see changed?
- What is the best praise you have ever received?
- Have you ever had any very productive partnerships? What do you believe made them work so well?
- Tell me about your future dreams and career goals.
- Is there anything else you want to talk about that might make us work better together?
- Let me tell you how I like to be updated.

Perfect Phrases to Handle Questions You Can't Answer

- Let me check on that and get back to you.

- I don't know, but I'll find out.

- That is something I haven't learned yet. Do you want me to find out for you or do you have another place to get that information?

- That is a decision I want to make myself. I will need to get more information before I do that, however.

- In my previous job, this is how we handled it. I'm not familiar with the procedure here yet.

- I am not convinced one way or another. I am going to wait until [date] to make a decision.

- I do not have a decision today. I will let you know as soon as I have gathered enough information to decide.

- That information is confidential. What I can tell you is …. (This is intended for information that truly is confidential. It is not intended for use when you do not know the answer.)

- I will be answering that question once the information is available.

- I could only provide a partial answer at this time. It would be better for me to wait until I have the complete response for you.

Perfect Phrases to Establish Yourself with Your Boss

Sometimes your own boss will need a little nudge to allow you to do the job you were hired to do.

- What advice do you have for me as a new manager?

- I want to free your time up as much as possible. To do that I suggest _____.

- I need my team members to come to me directly in order to supervise effectively. Will you encourage them to do that?

- Can I count on you to refer my staff members back to me when they come to you with a request I haven't authorized?

- Can I count on you to refer my staff members back to me when they come to you with questions I can answer?

- What assignments do you want me to take off your plate?

- I assume you want my team members to report to me now instead of you. Are there any situations where you want them to come directly to you?

- Am I free to make decisions about _____ without consulting you?

Perfect Phrases for Handling Employees Who Think They Are in Charge

Sometimes you need Perfect Phrases to establish your authority with those who think they are or should be in charge.

- I understand you have strong ideas about how this should be done. I'd like to hear them before I make my decision. Your input is important, and it is my decision to make.

- Why do you think it is appropriate to go over my head?

- I appreciate your expertise in this area. However, the success or failure of this project rests with me, and that is why I expect to make the final decision about this.

- Please tell my why you thought it was appropriate to take that action without consulting me.

- I am aware that I am new and may not have earned your respect yet. However, I will not accept insubordination. If you have problems with a directive, I am happy to discuss your issues. Otherwise, I expect your cooperation. Is there anything you see as unreasonable about that?

- I made the decision to do it this way because it has worked in the past. Until we come up with a better way, I need you to follow this procedure. Will you agree?

- You have some great ideas and I would like you on the team to come up with a better solution. Until then, everyone needs to do it this way, including you.

- Here are the situations where I expect you to make the decisions: _____. Here are the situations where I expect you to defer to me: _____.

Perfect Phrases to Introduce Hands-on Involvement

It is important to familiarize yourself with the jobs your employees do. Use Perfect Phrases to introduce the practice to shadow your employees in a way that minimizes resistance.

- I will be shadowing you in your work occasionally. It is not to check *up* on you; it is to check *in* with you.

- I understand you have been working on your own. My goal is to learn what I can to help you do your job, to find out how I can support you.

- You are the expert—you do this every day. I want to learn from the expert.

- The more I understand about your job, the better I will be able to help you.

- A manager once told me, "If you want to learn how to do a job, go to the people who do it." I'd like to learn from you.

Perfect Phrases to Announce Changes Gracefully

Since people tend to resist change, it is essential that you choose the words to announce change well.

- I am committed to keeping you informed about any decision that affects you in any way.

- I have some changes to announce. Let me tell you what is changing, when, and why. I will tell you whom it will affect and how much control we will have over the changes.

- I am aware this is different from how we have been operating. Let me explain why it will benefit us all.

- Now that you have heard this latest news, what are your thoughts and feelings about it?

- What do you understand the changes to be and how will they affect you?

- I have shared what information I have. I will do my best to get answers to the questions that remain.

- I am aware of the following rumors. I want to address them all.

- Please pass on to me any rumors that you hear, so I can clarify the situation.

Perfect Phrases to Handle Resistance to Change

- I am about to announce a change. I am aware that the first response to change is usually resistance. I encourage you be aware of any resistance and to give this change the chance to succeed.

- Like any change, this one will probably feel awkward at first. Once you are used to it, I believe it will feel more natural than what we are doing now.

- Let me tell you what's at stake here.

- Resisting change is *normal!* We all do it to some degree—even me. My goal is not to defeat resistance. My goal is to help us all move through the resistance, accept this change, and become more productive as a result.

- I want your suggestions to help us all get through this transition and make it as easy as possible.

- Here are the problems we are experiencing. If we do not solve the problem ourselves, upper management will dictate changes. Let's make our own changes.

- I know some of you are resisting this change and I understand that. We must implement this change and I need you all behind it. How can we do that?

- I know how you feel. When I first heard about this change, I had some doubts, too. But now that I understand the goal, I see how it's going to work. Let me explain.

Perfect Phrases to Support a Change You Don't Agree With

If it hasn't happened yet, it's going to. You will be asked to implement a change you don't agree with completely or maybe not at all. That doesn't necessarily mean it's a bad idea. As a manager, you must support management decisions. If you disagree, express your opinion directly to your supervisor. Express your support to your team with these Perfect Phrases:

■ Management has decided to make this change and, as part of the management team, I support it.

■ I understand your frustration. This change will create more work for you. Let me explain why it is necessary.

■ This is what has been decided and this is what we're going to do.

■ I know this is difficult. In this case we don't have a choice, so this is what we're going to do.

Chapter 3
Perfect Phrases to Create a Mission-, Vision-, and Values-Based Team

People burn out more from a lack of sense of purpose than from a lack of energy.[1] The leader who guides employees to answer the questions "Why are we here?" and "What are we trying to do?" with heartfelt answers they can commit to, will have a smooth-running team. If the leader helps the team establish a shared vision of purpose, the team will move in the same direction. A team with shared values is a team of people who can work together to get the job done. If the mission, vision, and values are well-defined, you will establish them in the minds and hearts of your team members. The mission, vision, and values will guide daily decisions and will foster commitment and involvement.

When I speak on this topic in management seminars, I see many in my audience roll their eyes, groan, and slouch back in

[1] *The Leadership Challenge*, 3rd Ed., James M. Kouzes and Barry Z. Posner, (San Francisco, Jossey-Bass, 2002), p. 55.

their chairs. These are managers who work for companies that have mission statements in name only. Few are following the mission and most don't even know it.

The experience of one company that had a well-thought-out mission statement is common. The executive committee spent a lot of time developing the values, goals, and mission of the company. When it was complete, they posted it on every bulletin board. One of the primary values listed was respect—we respect our clients, our vendors, and our co-workers. However, one of the executives who helped write the mission statement believed in management by intimidation. He yelled at his staff during meetings, sometimes yelled at clients, and was rude to vendors. None of the employees believed in the mission. They reasoned that if the value of respect were truly part of the mission, the executive would not be allowed to behave that way.

Your mission statement won't serve its purpose, which is to unite the team through common goals and values, unless you apply it. If you're not prepared to walk the talk, don't write it. You will do more harm than good.

If you are willing to commit to principles and standards to manage by, use the following Perfect Phrases help you draw out the common mission, vision, and values of your team. The phrases to establish mission, vision, and values are provided primarily for the purpose of brainstorming. That's why most of the phrases are in the form of questions.

Perfect Phrases to Establish Mission

Your mission defines the purpose of your team, department, or organization. For example, the mission of my organization, SpeakStrong, Inc., is "To increase awareness of the need for truthfulness personally, professionally and politically throughout the world community: To provide individuals with the tools and courage to speak their Simple Truth." That mission is the reason why SpeakStrong, Inc. exists.

If your organization has a mission statement, be certain to reinforce it. Get the team to help you define your team vision by asking the following questions.

- What do you see as our top priority?

- What are we here to accomplish?

- Why is this [team / department / organization] important?

- What makes us great?

- What makes us unique?

- What is our greatest contribution to the [world / customers / company]?

- What do our customers really want from us?

- If our customers wrote our mission statement, what would it say?

- What do you like about our company?

- In what ways are your interests not represented?

- Considering the input, what would you say our mission is?

- How can we rank these missions?

- Which of these missions is the highest priority?
- Is this a mission you can believe in?
- What would make it more relevant for you?

Perfect Phrases to Establish Vision

Your vision is your picture of possibilities for the organization or unit. For example, the vision of SpeakStrong is "To make SpeakStrong and PowerPhrases a household word: To become the leading communication experts internationally." This is the vision we strive for.

Use these phrases to encourage your team to form a shared vision.

- Here is my picture of what we can do. What pictures do you have?

- How do you see us at our best?

- If we could become whatever we wanted and we knew we could not fail, what would we look like?

- Realistically, what can we envision?

- Where are you personally in that picture?

- Tell me more.

- If you could change anything, what would it be?

- How does your vision for yourself blend with your vision for the company?

- What are you willing to do to make this vision happen?

- Are you willing to commit to this vision?

- How would you rank the proposed visions?

- Which visions inspire you more?

Perfect Phrases to Establish Values

A value is a principle, standard, or quality considered worthwhile or desirable. For example, the SpeakStrong values are truth, courage, open communication, and respect. Those are the values we observe in everything we do.

Most companies have stated values. If your company has stated values, be certain to reinforce those values as well as reinforcing values for your immediate team. Use these Perfect Phrases to determine team values. How people prioritize work depends on what values matter most. If you have conflict, it could be a result of different values.

- What values are essential for our mission and vision?
- What values do we hold in common?
- What matters most: quality, service, or price?
- What do you like about our [products/services]?
- What don't you like about our [products/services]?
- What makes work worth doing for you?
- Name two people you admire and two qualities they each embody.
- Are there any values you would be willing to die for?
- What does it mean to work here?
- What do you want it to mean?
- What qualities do you believe should drive our business?
- Which of these values are most important?
- What values are we willing to commit to?

Perfect Phrases to Make the Mission, Vision, and Values Real

After you have used the information gathered to formulate your mission, vision, and values, use more Perfect Phrases to make those values real. It does not matter how powerful your vision, mission, and values are if they aren't put into practice. As a manager, you need to reinforce the statements on a regular basis by referring to them as a matter of course.

- This initiative is in alignment with our mission because ….

- If we are serious about our vision, this (project, idea, decision) will help us by ….

- Since our top value is _____, how do you think we should handle the incongruity in this [decision / reallocation / etc.]?

- Which decision best fulfills our mission?

- Which direction best fulfills our vision?

- Which decision best represents our values?

- How will we show we are committed to our mission?

- What will we do to show we are committed to our mission?

- How will we show we are committed to our vision?

- What will we do to show we are committed to our vision?

- How will we show we are committed to our values?

- What will we do to show we are committed to our values?

- Let me remind you why we are here.
- This behavior is not consistent with our mission.
- Don't forget what our mission is.

To use these phrases with integrity, you need to have a personal investment in the mission, vision, and values. If you are personally committed and you let your commitment show, magic can happen. Your staff will internalize them as well, and their decisions will be guided as if you were there.

Chapter 4
Perfect Phrases to Foster an Open Communication Culture

Communication is two-way by definition. For communication to occur, it is essential that employees feel safe to speak freely. Yet how often does that happen? Only 6% of employees report feeling safe questioning instructions and directives.[1] As a result, bad ideas go unchallenged and good ideas often never get heard. Employees have difficulty saying no to projects that overload their schedule. When employees do not feel safe speaking freely, they often hesitate to question directions when needed and they make up what they don't understand.

Whether the people you supervise feel safe speaking up or asking questions depends largely on you. There are many ways to discourage disclosure without realizing it. Ridiculing an idea, becoming defensive if criticism is directed against you, and retaliating against someone who was forthright with you sends a message throughout the team that it is not safe to speak. There

[1] Working Values Web site, www.workingvalues.com.

is a price to be paid for a dynamic of silence.

This chapter is based on the following five SpeakStrong and Center for Responsible Communication principles:

1. Open communication is essential for health personally, professionally, and politically.
2. When any communication is suppressed, it is unhealthy for all involved and is likely to come back and cost everyone.
3. We need to elevate the level of discourse personally, professionally, and politically.
4. We have a right to be informed about things that affect us.
5. When we don't speak up, we are complicit with lies, poor decisions, and deception.

The benefits of an open communication culture are manifold. Employees feel safe, and as a manager you can feel safe as well, knowing that you will not be faced with unpleasant surprises. Problems can be addressed before they become major issues. You will have the benefit of ideas from people who have a different perspective than you do. It will create buy-in among employees.

Choose your Perfect Phrases with care to ensure that your words inspire disclosure rather than suppression.

Perfect Phrases to Ensure That You Are Kept in the Loop

- If you ever wonder if you should tell me something or not or cc me on something or not, go ahead and do it.

- Please inform me of any changes regarding _____. The following is a list of areas I do not need to be informed of: _____.

- Is there anything going on I might want to know?

- I trust your expertise in your own areas. I need to be updated to stay in the loop myself.

- I want to check in with you, not check up on you.

- I am committed to letting you know anything that affects you. Please be certain to let me know anything that affects me as the supervisor and the group as a whole.

- Please give us an update of your progress by _____.

- Is the project running on schedule?

- Is everything within budget?

- Are the quality specifications being met?

- What can I do to support your work?

- I was not informed about _____. In the future, please update me about events such as these.

- My boss said you came directly to him with this issue. I am concerned that you went over my head, but I'm more concerned about our relationship. What made you think you couldn't come to me first?

Perfect Phrases to Encourage Feedback

- Let's find the best way to get this done.
- If you did have an objection to this initiative, what would it be?
- Please tell me what you like about this [plan/procedure/idea/etc.]. What would make you like it more?
- What do you believe could conceivably go wrong with this in the worst possible scenario?
- What do you think of this? You don't have to be right.
- Do you see a better way of doing this?
- What do I, we, or you need to know to make this endeavor successful?
- What have I overlooked?

Perfect Phrases to Encourage Questions on Policies and Directives

- Please ask three questions about my instructions. If we are making any assumptions, I'd like to find out now.

- I want to make sure my instructions are clear. What is your understanding of what I just said?

- What did I leave out?

- What would you like reviewed?

- What will your first step be?

- What questions do you have?

- What ideas do you have about _____? I feel like I'm missing something. Is there something you want to tell me?

- Please take a moment and summarize our discussion so far.

- What main points stand out in what we said?

- Let's see if I communicated well. What did you hear me say?

- I want to make sure we are headed in the same direction. Where do you plan to start?

Perfect Phrases to Get a Quiet Employee to Open Up

- I've noticed your interest in _____. I'm interested as well.

- I've noticed your interest in _____. Tell me about it.

- I find there are some employees who share everything that happens and others who stay pretty reserved. I know it's tough to speak when others are so outspoken. I invite you to open up to me.

- I used to hold back from talking to my boss because I didn't know if it was safe. I want you to feel safe talking to me, and I invite you to test me.

- If you won't talk to me, I won't be able to support or manage you.

- We can't do this alone. Your input is crucial.

- I can't work with unspoken issues between us. I need to clear the air.

- This is not personal. This affects our ability to do our jobs. I need to know where you stand on this.

- I often find the quietest employees are quiet because they are so thoughtful and the ones who speak the least are the ones who have the most to say. What's on your mind?

- There is a saying, "Still waters run deep." I'm guessing that's the case with you. I think you have some deep thoughts on what's going on. How can I get you to open up?

Perfect Phrases to Encourage Employees to Communicate Directly and Effectively with Each Other

- Who do you think needs to be informed of changes regarding _____?

- Let's make a list of all the stakeholders in this [issue / project / initiative] so you can update them about developments.

- What information do you think would be necessary to share?

- Have you spoken with [employee with whom they have an issue] about this?

- I expect you and [employee with whom they have an issue] to communicate. If you need my help, I'm happy to support you. However, I won't do it for you.

- I understand there is some gossip happening here. I will not tolerate that. I expect you to speak about people in the same way you would if they were there and to bring all issues to the person involved.

- I expect you to tell someone attempting to gossip with you to bring the issues directly to the person involved.

Perfect Phrases to Encourage Employees to Admit Mistakes

Employees who are afraid to admit mistakes can be very costly. Check your reactions when employees tell you about problems and mistakes, because if you are discouraging truthfulness about errors, it could result in some very costly surprises.

- Mistakes are learning experiences. Let me tell you about a mistake I made.

- When you make a mistake, I want to hear about it immediately. I also will want to hear what you learned and what you will do in the future to keep from making that mistake again.

- Mistakes are inevitable and acceptable. Hiding mistakes is not.

- I believe most people come to work wanting to do their best. When a member of my team makes a mistake, it is usually because I haven't given him or her proper training, support, direction, or encouragement. Please tell me when you make a mistake so I can help us both do our jobs better.

- I will never yell at anyone who makes a mistake.

- I want you to make mistakes. When you make mistakes, it tells me you're thinking, you're making decisions, and you're taking risks.

- I want you to make mistakes. I don't want poor performance.

Perfect Phrases to Promote Diversity

- I've heard some rumors about the team not accepting our [new/minority/handicapped] employee. What's going on?

- I'd like some input on how we're doing welcoming all cultures. Give it some thought and let's meet next week.

- As you know, we have a nondiscrimination policy. What have you seen or heard that I need to know about?

- I've heard that you have been critical of [name]'s work, saying that wasn't a job for someone of that [race/gender/etc.]. Are these stories true?

- According to the law and our company manual, discrimination is prohibited. The protected classes I'm particularly concerned about are [Hispanics / blacks / homosexuals / handicapped]. In order to encourage an open discussion, I invite you to come to my office and talk any time something bothers you.

- We all have prejudices. I expect you to set those feelings aside while you are here. I expect you to treat everyone fairly and courteously regardless of race, religion, color, or sexual preference.

- I have heard of some discriminating behavior. I don't expect you to talk about it in a public forum, but I want you to know I'm paying attention. Within the next week, I would like each of you to come to my office individually to discuss any issues.

- I will not tolerate discrimination in any form. I will document anything I witness or hear from others.

- As I look around the room, I see many cultures and races. I am grateful for this diversity, because your various backgrounds and ways of thinking help us solve problems.

- I'm open to hearing any thoughts—even negative thoughts—about our diversity policy. It is only by talking about these issues and bringing them into the open that we can solve them and move on to what's important—doing the best work we can.

- Gender-neutral terms allow all members of this team to contribute.

- That type of [behavior / entertainment / activity] excludes some of the cultures here, so we need to find an alternative that is inclusive.

Perfect Phrases to Encourage Employees to Resolve Conflict

■ You two have been arguing for some time. I would like you both to meet in the conference room now and come up with a plan to work this out. Let me know what you decide.

■ Both of you have strong opinions and I respect both sides of the issue. Please write up the strengths of your opinions and meet to discuss them.

■ I notice tension between you. Would you like me to facilitate a problem-solving discussion?

■ I need you to come up with a way to work together or I will solve the problem for you. I would rather you solve it.

■ By Monday I want you to come up with 10 things you agree on.

■ You two don't have to like each other, but you do have to find a way to work together. Please let me know by Friday how you plan to do this.

■ Your arguing is negatively affecting the entire group. What do you intend to do to about it?

■ It is not realistic to think we will like everyone we work with. But we do have to treat everyone respectfully and professionally. Do you two believe you're doing that?

■ I suspect something is going on between you two. Do you want to talk about it with me or work it out on your own?

- Avoiding conflict does not make it go away. Please go into the conference room and put your issues on the table.

- I want to hear both of you describe the problem, from the other person's perspective. How do you think he or she would describe the problem?

Perfect Phrases to Invite Feedback About Your Performance as Manager

Nothing opens up communication as quickly as being open to feedback. Employees respect a leader who invites, listens to, and learns from feedback.

- Do you think I am an effective communicator?
- In what ways am I effective in communicating with you and the team?
- In what ways am I ineffective in communicating with you and the team?
- Do I listen well when others talk?
- Am I perceived as caring or abrasive?
- What things am I doing right that you would like me to continue doing?
- There is something that is bothering you. Talk to me about it and what I can do.
- In order to manage, I need feedback on how I am doing. Please tell me where you believe I am strong and where I can do better.
- I may do some things that are perceived as [rude / abrupt / abrasive / curt] without realizing it myself. Can you think of things I do?
- When I improve as a manager, your job gets easier. I can't improve without feedback. I am sincerely asking you for honesty about how to improve with the team.
- Please tell me how I am a good manager and where I

am falling short. I promise there will be no reprisal for anything you say.

- This takes courage, but I'm going to ask the question anyway. What can I do better?

Chapter 5
Perfect Phrases to
Ace the Interview
You Conduct

One of the most important decisions you make as a manager is the decision about whom to hire. Hiring the wrong person can be devastating for you, your entire team, and the person you hire. How can you know if the person sitting across from you is the answer to your prayer or your worst nightmare?

This chapter provides perfect interview phrases to successfully … and legally … learn what you need to know before you commit to the wrong person. Pick your words with care, knowing what information you are looking for with every question you ask.

Perfect Phrases to Learn Facts and Personal Information

The phrases in this section are designed to determine if the candidate's situation and background are appropriate for the job and to obtain the information you need without getting you into legal trouble. Rather than asking about age, citizenship, family situation, and health situation, use the Perfect Phrases below to get the information you really want—whether the candidate can do the job you need him or her to do.

- Do you have legal verification of your right to work in this country?

- What languages do you speak, read, or write?

- These are the hours, days, and shifts that are to be worked. Is there anything that would interfere with your ability to work these hours?

- If we hire you, do you have proof of your age?

- Are you comfortable with our policy of not allowing personal phone calls at work?

- Is there anything that keeps you from being able to _____?

- This job requires lifting 50 lbs. Can you lift 50 lbs.?

- Tell me about the most physically demanding job you have had.

Perfect Phrases to Learn Work Styles and Preferences

These questions are designed to find out how the candidate likes to work.

- Do you prefer working alone or in groups?
- What kind of people do you find it hard to work with? Why?
- Do you like a lot of involvement or independence?
- What are some things you like to avoid in a job? Why?
- What would you say is the most important thing you are looking for in a job?
- What were some of the things about your last job that you found most challenging?
- What are some things you liked best about your last job?
- How do you feel about the way your last supervisor managed you?
- Why are you leaving your present job? (or) Why did you leave your last job?
- What is important to you in a company? What things do you look for in an organization?
- How much supervision are you used to?
- I see you worked at _____ from _____ to _____. Why did you choose that firm?
- What is the most important quality a person in this position should have?

Perfect Phrases to Learn Work Expectations

These questions are designed to uncover how the candidate perceives the job for which he or she is applying.

- What about the ad for this job caught your interest?
- Where do you see yourself in five years?
- What is your ideal job? How do you see this position compared with that ideal?
- Why are you applying for this position?
- How did you hear about this position?

Perfect Phrases to Learn Work Perceptions

These questions show the level of the candidate's perceptiveness.

- Tell me about myself. (Yes, you read it right. The purpose is to assess the candidate's judgment of character.)
- Did you draw any conclusions about the company from the application?
- Was there anything about the application you would recommend changing?
- What has your experience with the company taught you so far?
- Describe the conference room where you waited.
- Do you recall the receptionist's name?

Perfect Situation-Specific Questions

These questions address the candidate's approach to situations he or she is likely to experience.

- What would you do to increase consumer widget awareness?

- When two managers insist that you give their projects priority, how do you handle it?

- This job calls for _____. What is your experience in this?

- This job requires _____. Tell me about your experience in this area.

Perfect Phrases to Learn Interpersonal Skills

If interpersonal skills are important, these questions will uncover how a candidate would handle the kinds of interpersonal challenges he or she is likely to face.

- Tell me about a time a customer was offensive or obnoxious and how you handled it.

- Describe a situation where you were tempted to lose your temper with a dissatisfied customer.

- Have you ever lost your temper with a customer or co-worker?

- Tell me about a time when you turned an angry customer around.

- Describe a situation where you went the extra mile to satisfy a tough customer.

- Describe a situation where you needed to refuse an unreasonable request from your boss.

- If your boss offended you, how would you handle it?

Perfect Phrases to Determine Self-Directedness and Personal Motivation

- Tell me about an obstacle you had to overcome and how you handled it.

- What have you done to prepare yourself to work in this field?

- How do you decide how to organize your time?

- What have you done in the past when you've realized an area of your work needed improvement?

- What are some of the obstacles you found in doing previous jobs? How did you handle them?

- How do you keep up with what's going on in [your company/your industry/your profession]?

- How many nonfiction books have you read in the last year?

- How important is it to you to be the best?

Perfect Phrases to Determine Leadership Qualities

These questions are designed to determine whether the candidate waits for others to guide or fills in a leadership gap where needed. They also are designed to see if the candidate considers the big picture or not.

- How do you get results from people you have no control over?

- Have you taken a management development course?

- How are you helping your subordinates/co-workers develop themselves?

- In your present job, how do you get people together to establish a common approach to a problem?

- What approach do you take in getting people to accept your ideas or department goals?

- What specifically do you do to set an example for others?

- What sort of leader do your people feel you are? Are you satisfied with that?

- How do you get people who do not want to work together to get along?

- What is your leadership style? Give examples.

- Do you work more effectively one to one or in a group?

- If you were the president of this company, what is one new [policy/plan/product] you would initiate?

- How do you motivate other people?

- Give an example of how you once saw a need and filled it.
- Do you see every employee as having a leadership role in an organization?

Perfect Phrases to Determine Experience

This section supplements the Perfect Situation-Specific Questions to determine whether the candidate has relevant experience.

- What work experience prepared you for this job?

- Tell me one or two things you have accomplished that you are proud of.

- What is one of your biggest disappointments in your work history?

- What kind of awards have you received for work performance?

- What would your previous staff and/or bosses say about you?

Perfect Phrases to Determine Education and Training

Not all relevant learning shows up on a standard interview form. These questions uncover learning that may not fit a standard job application.

- What education or training has prepared you for this job?
- What classes have you taken that have been of most help in doing your job?
- What else has provided you with knowledge useful for this job?
- What has been the most important person or event in your self-development?
- How much education have you earned?
- What kinds of books and other publications do you read?

Perfect Phrases to Determine Career Goals

If an employee's career goals match the opportunities you offer, the employee is more likely to be motivated. Find out with the questions listed below.

- What is your long-term employment or career objective?

- How do you see this job fitting with that objective?

- What skills and knowledge will you need to do that?

- Why do you believe you will be successful doing that?

- If you had this job, what would you like to accomplish?

- What might make you leave this job?

- What would cause you to stay for a long time?

Perfect Phrases to Determine Self-Assessment

How does this candidate see himself or herself? It can be useful to find out. The questions below probe gently into attitudes that may be useful to know in advance.

- Everyone has strengths and weaknesses as workers. What are your strong points for this job?

- Was your progress on your previous job representative of your ability? Why or why not?

- What do you think are the most important success skills? Do you have them?

- Do you consider yourself to be innovative?

- What satisfies you at work?

- What frustrates you at work? How do you deal with it?

- What are your strengths?

- Why should I hire you?

- What are you most proud about in your previous job?

- What makes you the best candidate?

Perfect Phrases to Determine Creativity

Creativity can be a valuable asset in most situations. However, it can be a liability if you have a highly creative person in a job that is very routine. Find out about the creativity of your applicant with the Perfect Phrases below.

- In your work experience, what have you done that you consider truly creative?

- Can you think of a time when the way things were done didn't work too well and you found a new way?

- What kinds of problems do people call on you to solve?

- If you were me trying to decide whether to hire you, what would you do?

Perfect Phrases to Determine Decisiveness

The Perfect Phrases below help you to know about the way your job candidate makes decisions and how comfortable he or she is in doing so.

■ Do you consider yourself to be systematic and analytical or do you usually make up your mind fast? Give an example. (Watch the time the candidate takes to respond.)

■ What was your toughest decision in the last six months? Why was it hard?

■ How do you make important decisions that affect your career?

■ How do you solve problems?

■ If a crisis occurred that your boss needed to make an immediate decision on but you couldn't reach him or her, what would you do?

Perfect Phrases to Determine Motivation

Find out how the candidate is motivated with the questions below.

- What motivates you?
- Tell me about a time you were highly motivated.
- What dampens motivation for you?
- Can you give me examples of experiences on the job that you felt were satisfying?
- What goals did you achieve last year?
- Describe how you prioritize your work.
- Can you give an example of a time when you saw a need and filled it without being asked to do so?

Perfect Phrases to Determine Work Standards

Some workers take "ownership" of projects and are committed to a successful outcome. Others are just "doing a job" and do not have an attitude of doing what it takes. Find out your candidate's approach.

- How do you measure success in your job?
- Do you expect to leave work exactly on time every day?
- How many sick days do you consider acceptable?
- In your position, how would you define doing a good job?
- When evaluating the performance of others, what factors or characteristics are most important to you?

Perfect Phrases to Determine Presentation Skills

- Do you like to speak in public?
- How do you prepare for presentations?
- What do you see as being essential to a good presentation?
- What is your greatest skill as a presenter?
- What tips do you think are essential for presenters?

Perfect Phrases to Determine Written Communication Skills

■ Would you rather write a report or give a verbal report? Why?

■ What kind of writing have you done? For a group? For an individual?

■ What major reports have you written?

■ What do you see as essential for a good written report?

Perfect Phrases to Determine Flexibility

Most jobs require flexibility. If the one for which you are interviewing does as well, these Perfect Phrases will determine if your candidate has the flexibility you require.

- What was the most important idea or suggestion you received recently? Did you change anything as a result?

- How do you handle constant changes in company operating policies and procedures?

- What was the most significant change made in a company you worked for? How successfully did you implement this change?

- When you're in the middle of a project and your boss calls with an immediate request, how do you handle it?

Perfect Phrases to Determine Stress Tolerance

- Do you get stressed at work? Tell me about it.

- What has been the highest-pressure situation you have been under in recent years? How did you cope with it?

- How well do you handle tight deadlines?

- Do you have a way of managing your stress?

Perfect Multipurpose Interview Sentence Stems

Whatever information you seek, your best questions will be open-ended. Use the Perfect Phrases below.

- What ...?
- Explain ....
- Describe ....
- How would you ...?
- In what ways ...?
- Under what circumstance do you ...?
- If you could ...?
- Please cite some examples of ....
- Tell me about ....

Chapter 6
Perfect Phrases
for Orientation

There is an old proverb that says, "Well begun is half done." The message is accurate. Another proverb that conveys a similar message is "A stitch in time saves nine." Expectations need to be communicated effectively the first time from the very first day. Orientation too often consists of showing the new employee his or her workspace and running off to fight a fire or resolve a crisis. Since you never get a second chance at a first impression, use Perfect Phrases to help the new employee feel welcome and oriented.

Perfect Phrases to Greet and Welcome

- We are glad you are here because ….

- We were pleased when you accepted this position because ….

- We're sure you are going to like it here.

- We are looking forward to having someone here with your experience in _____.

- Let me introduce you. This is _____ and [he/she] is responsible for _____.

Perfect Phrases to Create Safety and Reassure the New Employee

- We know what it's like to be new, and we're here to help the transition go smoothly.

- We have the following measures to help you through the inevitable learning curve.

- When you get stuck, here's what you do.

- When you need help, this is whom you turn to.

- What questions do you have now?

Perfect Phrases to Introduce the New Employee to the Company

- The history, mission, and goals of the [department/company] are ….

- Let me show you the organizational chart.

- Here's where you can get more information on our history, mission, vision, and goals. Most employees [are / aren't] familiar with them.

- The employee handbook is a great source of information for you. Please review it, and then I will highlight the most relevant policies.

- Here is the operating manual from the person who had the job before you. I expect it will be useful, and I also know you will develop your own approaches.

- To get your ID card, you need to ….

- Benefits information is available through _____.

- The security information you need is ….

- If you have any safety concerns or injuries, contact _____.

- The parking info you need is ….

Perfect Phrases to Reinforce Disciplinary Policies

- We require our employees to dress according to the following dress code ….

- Our absenteeism policy is as follows ….

- As our manual states, employment here is at will. That means either one of us can end the employment at any time.

- Should you ever need to file a grievance, this manual tells you how.

- Our policy about proprietary information is ….

- Other key policies that all employees need to know before starting their jobs are ….

Perfect Phrases to Get the New Employee Started

- What I want you to do now is ….

- If you need me, the best time and the best way to reach me are ….

- Your job responsibilities are ….

- I will fill you in on your initial job responsibilities when we meet [date and time].

- Your workdays and hours are _____. Is that what you expected?

- Please review your position description and we will discuss expectations and standards.

- Your position description provides the framework and essential job duties for your scope of responsibility.

- The position description provides clarity on priorities and helps you understand how you will be evaluated.

- We will meet to discuss the details [date and time].

Perfect Phrases to Establish Feedback

- Plan to meet with me [weekly / daily / twice weekly / etc.] for the first six months.

- Regular meetings provide an opportunity to clear up misunderstandings, obtain feedback, clarify priorities, and develop an effective working relationship.

- Feedback will be important for me to manage you and for you to do your job. It is important for us to be completely honest with each other about how things are going.

- My goal is to empower you to handle issues on your own as soon as possible. In the beginning, you can expect a high level of involvement. You can expect that level to decrease as you learn the ropes.

- Initially, if you have any questions about _____, bring them to me and let me decide.

- Initially, if you have any questions about _____, bring them to me and we'll decide how to handle it.

- If you have any questions about _____, decide what needs to be done and let me know what you have decided.

- If you have any questions or issues with _____, I will leave it to your discretion and I don't need to know about it.

- You are free to make decisions about _____ without consulting me.

- If you have any issues that require immediate attention, contact me by _____.
- The preferred times to reach me are [times]. If something needs immediate attention, contact me immediately.

Perfect Phrases to Introduce the New Employee to the Culture

- It is common office etiquette around here to [return calls within three hours / clean the coffeepot when less than one cup is left/etc.].

- The way people socialize around here is [birthday parties / social activities/etc.].

- Generally the culture is [casual/formal/driven/competitive/cooperative/etc.].

- Always cc [name] on anything related to _____.

- The standard format for letters and memos is .…

- A great way to build relationships among colleagues, supervisor, and staff is to .…

- Our company has a [softball / bowling/racquetball] team. All employees are welcome to participate. If you're interested, talk to [name].

Chapter 7
Perfect Phrases
for Delegation

Delegation—getting work done through others—is one of the most underused tools of managers. Of course it needs to be done well to get results. Good delegation phrases need to be clear, complete, accepted, and understood.

Perfect Phrases to Encourage Buy-in

Sure, it may be their job, but if employees are motivated they will do their job much better than if they are not. Use the phrases below to ensure that they will do their best, not because they have to, but because they want to.

- There is an opportunity here for you to ….

- I have a project I'm bringing to you because it's essential it's done right.

- I'm asking you because I know I can trust you.

- I am aware of how busy you are. However, I have a request.

- I would never ask you to do something I would not do myself.

- I have a project I can only trust my very best [rep / manager / engineer] with.

- I need your help.

- I have a project that is outside your usual area that I think you will enjoy.

Perfect Phrases to Express the Benefit of an Assignment

If you can offer a benefit, it often encourages buy-in.

- What this means to you is ….
- This will help you by ….
- If you do this for me, I will ….
- I'll make sure my boss knows how you made a difference when I really needed you.
- This will be good, not only for me and the team, but for you because ….

Perfect Phrases to Ensure Clarity in Delegation

Being certain to include the following elements in ensuring clarity of instructions can save tremendous amounts of time and avoid error.

- I need _____ by _____ because _____.
- Here is what needs to happen.
- I have written out instructions. Let's go over them together.
- The deadline is _____.
- The quality specifications are ….
- The budget is _____.
- Of these three, the priority in this project is _____.
- An example of what it will look like is ….

Perfect Phrases to Ensure Understanding of an Assignment

Once you have explained an assignment, use Perfect Phrases to make sure that employees understand what you mean.

- What questions do you have at this point?

- What did I leave out?

- What would you like reviewed?

- What will your first step be?

- Let me make sure my instructions are clear. What is your understanding of what I have told you?

- What questions remain?

- What ideas do you have about _____?

- What do you think about _____?

- If you were required to question this assignment, what questions would you have?

Perfect Phrases to Elicit Input During Delegation

Don't assume that employees will tell you if they have a problem with your directives or will ask questions if it is unclear what you expect of them. Use Perfect Phrases to make sure.

- Do you see a better way of doing this?
- What do you see as a challenge here?
- Is there anything about this task that concerns or troubles you?
- Will your current workload allow you to complete this on time?

Perfect Phrases to Make Sure a Task Is Accepted

You may think when your delegate accepts a task you can count on him or her to complete it as expected. Don't be too certain. Be sure to use a Perfect Phrase to ensure acceptance.

- Can I count on you?

- When will you have that for me?

- I want a written plan by Tuesday.

- Let me know what a reasonable deadline for you is.

- Think about how this can be accomplished without sacrificing other priorities and let me know by _____.

- Let's pause for a minute and see if we both agree on

   _____.

- Is there anything that might interfere with getting this done?

- What do you need from me to be able to complete this?

- This is an important project and it's imperative that it's done right and on time. Are you OK with this?

- I am depending on you to do an excellent job and meet this deadline. How confident are you with this project?

Perfect Phrases to Eliminate Reverse Delegation

Even if you've never heard of reverse delegation, chances are you've experienced it. It's when you delegate a project and somehow it ends up back on your desk. Use these Perfect Phrases when someone attempts to pass an assignment back to you.

- I'll coach you through, but I won't do this for you. What do we need to go over?

- What have you tried so far?

- What have you considered that you haven't tried?

- Which part of the project do we need to discuss further to enable you to complete this on your own?

- What aspects of the project have I not made clear?

- Is there some training you need to complete this on your own?

- I'll help you when you are stuck, but I won't do it for you. I believe you can do this. Give it another try.

- This is a skill you need to master. It's a learning experience I want you to have. I am willing to invest the time in having you learn how to complete this project on your own.

- I gave you this assignment because I believe you will be good at it. I'm leaving it with you.

- This is not something I have time for. I need for you to move ahead with it.

Perfect Phrases to Refuse an Employee Request

■ I'd like to be able to do that for you. The reason why I can't is _____. Here is what I can do for you.

■ I agree it would be good to _____. The reason why I can't approve that is because ….

■ I know being able to [leave early / take personal calls / extend the deadline / etc.] is important to you. The reason why I can't approve it is ….

■ I appreciate your need for more money. At present your performance does not indicate a raise in pay. Let's look over your performance to see what would indicate a raise in the future.

Perfect Phrases to Credential Your Employees

Sometimes employees can be more effective if they are given your authority. If necessary, use those Perfect Phrases to be certain your delegate will get the cooperation he or she needs to be effective.

- When [name] asks for something, I expect you to give it to her.

- [Name] is in charge of [project]. Please give [him/her] your full cooperation.

- [Name] speaks for me.

- [Name] is working on an important project for me. Please give [his / her] requests the same priority you give mine.

- [Name] is taking over this project and has the authority to make decisions. Please refer questions to [him/her].

- I have given [name] the authority to run this project as [he / she] deems appropriate.

- If [name] asks you for help on this project, please make it your priority.

Perfect Phrases to Follow up on Delegated Projects

Never assume that your employees will tell you when they get behind schedule or that they will ask for help if they need it. They may not, which is why you need to schedule follow-up meetings at the time of delegation.

- Please give [us / me] an update of your progress.
- Is the project running on schedule?
- Is everything within budget?
- Are the quality specifications being met?
- What can I do to support your work?
- Can you envision anything that might interfere with your successful completion of this project?
- Are you getting the cooperation you need?
- Do you need any help to complete this on time?
- Are things working out the way we thought they would?

Chapter 8
Perfect Phrases to Set and Communicate Standards and Goals

The focus of this book is to provide phrases to communicate verbally. After providing phrases to set job standards, I include a sampling of job standards and performance goals in order to show what effective standards and goals sound like. For an exhaustive list of phrases for documenting job standards and performance goals, refer to *Perfect Phrases for Setting Performance Goals* by Douglas Max and Robert Bacal.

I also focus on how to communicate established standards and goals. How goals are communicated can make the difference between standards and goals that guide the day-to-day operations and standards and goals that are quickly forgotten.

Perfect Phrases to Set Job Standards

Job standards are the description of what you want the employee to do. They reflect the features of the job irrespective of who is holding it. They must focus on what the employee is to *do*, not what you want the employee to *be*. They must avoid ambiguity. Standards are in two categories: behavior and performance.

JOB STANDARDS—BEHAVIOR: EXAMPLES

- Make one personal comment to each customer per transaction.

- Deal with problems in a calm, helpful, and productive manner, without raising your voice, complaining, or using sarcasm.

- Deal constructively with conflict and in a manner that promotes cooperation and consensus building.

JOB STANDARDS—PERFORMANCE: EXAMPLES

- Develop and prepare forms, records, and charts to achieve effective workloads and workflow.

- Greet visitors, answer telephone calls and take messages, and open and sort mail directed to the [dean / director].

- Maintain appointment schedules and calendars. Make travel arrangements and arrange meetings. Assist in agenda preparation. Gather information and contact meeting participants.

Perfect Phrases to Gather Input to Identify Job Standards

Every employee needs to know what is expected of him or her, which means that as a manager you need to ensure that job standards are relevant. It begins by gathering input on the perfect standards.

When determining job standards, you will sometimes have a working model for a reference. Do not limit yourself to a previous description. My informal surveys indicate that about 50% of employees have job descriptions, but 80% of the time they do not reflect the actual position. To make job standards relevant, use Perfect Phrases to investigate what the job really entails. These are questions for the employees who already work in the position, for employees who held that position formerly, and for co-workers who depend upon and interact with the employees in that position.

Perfect Phrase Questions to Ask Employees Currently or Formerly in the Position to Determine Job Standards

- What is the main purpose of the job as you see it?
- What are the primary responsibilities of the job as you see them?
- What parts of the job are essential, such that there would be serious consequences if they were not done?
- What parts of the job are nonessential, but useful?
- What do others depend on this position for?
- What aspects of this job affect the mission and vision of the company? How?

Perfect Phrase Questions to Ask Those Who Depend on the Position to Determine Job Standards

- What do you depend on the person in this position for?
- What do you see as essential for this position?
- What qualities and behaviors do you appreciate most from the person in this position?
- What job standards would you like for the person in this position?

Perfect Phrases to Ensure Agreement to Job Standards

Employees sometimes agree to standards without giving them much thought. Use Perfect Phrases to ensure job standards and affirm commitment.

- Do these standards make sense to you?

- These standards are solid expectations, not suggestions of what it would be nice for you to do. Is there anything about these standards that you do not feel able to commit to?

- Is there any way you believe these standards need to be changed to make them more viable?

- Do you believe these standards define the essence of the job?

- Can you see how important it is to the company and the team mission and vision to fulfill these standards?

- Are you committed to these standards?

- How [will / do] you show your commitment to these standards?

- Our formal review is set for [date]. However, there is no need to wait for that date to discuss any questions you have about the standards, brainstorm ways to overcome obstacles, or realign the standards if necessary.

Perfect Phrases to Reinforce Job Standards

Sometimes standards will be set and forgotten. Make certain that does not happen; reinforce standards consistently. Standards will be the focus of performance reviews, but bring them up between reviews whenever it seems useful to reinforce them.

- Given the standards, we need to look at how you are doing.
- I think we need to review the standards again.
- Do you think you are meeting your standards and goals?
- Is there any confusion about what the standards are?
- I notice you are .… Let's go over the standards and see what needs to be changed in how you do your job.
- What I am asking for is not arbitrary. It is part of the basic standards for this position.
- This function is standard for the job.

Perfect Phrases to Negotiate Performance Goals

Performance goals are different from job standards. While anyone in a position is expected to meet the standards, performance goals are specific to the individual depending on his or her strengths and weaknesses. Goals create focus, inspiration, and motivation. The best goals are negotiated between the manager and the employee, using Perfect Phrases, of course.

■ Now that we have the standards outlined, let's create goals for you to aspire to.

■ The purpose of this meeting is for us to establish performance goals to give you focus, inspiration, and motivation.

■ The best goals are ones we collaborate on setting.

■ In what areas do you see room to do your job better than the standards call for?

■ Although your job standards in the area of _____ are _____, I believe you are capable of more. Do you agree?

■ What strengths would you like to develop?

■ What specifically can you do to improve those skills?

■ I recommend you improve those skills by _____.

■ How would improving those skills directly enhance your job?

■ How would it benefit the company for you to target a higher standard in that area?

- How will we measure success?

- Here is how I will measure success.

- This goal is set to be achieved by _____.

- Our next formal review is set for [date]. However, there is no need to wait for that date to discuss any questions you have, brainstorm ways to achieve the goals, or realign the goals if necessary.

PERFORMANCE GOALS—BEHAVIOR: EXAMPLES

Like job standards, performance goals also come in two categories: behavioral goals and results goals. (For an exhaustive list of phrases for documenting job standards and performance goals, refer to *Perfect Phrases for Setting Performance Goals* by Douglas Max and Robert Bacal.)

- Be more customer-friendly. Smile at customers at least once per contact.

- Improve listening skills. Repeat back what speaker is saying at least five times per day.

- Learn more about the cultures represented here by reading two books.

- Eliminate the use of sarcasm. When you catch yourself using it, repeat the sentence without it.

PERFORMANCE GOALS—RESULTS: EXAMPLES

- Become more precise in responses to inquiries by including more details.

- Decrease errors in invoices by 35%.

- Answer phones more promptly, by the third ring.

- Increase sales volume by 20%.

Perfect Phrases to Ensure Agreement to Performance Goals

Employees sometimes agree to goals without giving them much thought. Sometimes they will set themselves up for failure by being too ambitious. Other times they will commit without taking them seriously. Use Perfect Phrases to confirm performance goals and affirm commitment.

- Do these performance goals make sense to you?
- Is there anything about these performance goals that you do not feel able to commit to?
- Is there any way you believe these performance goals need to be changed to make them more viable?
- Do you believe these performance goals are relevant to the essence of the job?
- Can you see how achieving these performance goals is important to the company and the team mission and vision?
- Are you committed to these performance goals?
- How [will/do] you show your commitment to these performance goals?
- Will you put your commitment to these goals in writing?

Chapter 9
Perfect Phrases to
Coach Employees

Many managers regard themselves as mentors to their employees. As such, they see coaching as a part of their responsibility to their employees. Coaching is not necessarily a disciplinary role. It is well used with your best employees as a way to develop their potential. Gallup research confirms that employees are happiest when their managers take a personal interest in them and their skills are put to good use. Use Perfect Phrases to ensure this.

Perfect Phrases for Informal Interaction

Feedback should not be limited to the performance review. "Managing by walking around" is recommended to create a presence in the workplace and to offer the opportunity for casual feedback. Check in with employees and offer feedback and support casually and informally as well as formally.

- How's it going?
- What's on your mind?
- Hey, I like the way you _____!
- It's always great to see you.
- By the way, great job on _____.
- I don't know how you do that, but I'm sure glad you do!
- What's going on?
- Are you getting the help you need?
- Is there anything you need from me?
- How comfortable is your workload?
- Is there anything you want me to know?
- Is there anything I can do to help you with the WidgetsRUs Project?
- How was your weekend?
- In the future I'd prefer ....

Perfect Phrases to Uncover Employee Strengths

It is confirmed by Gallup that the best managers build on the areas in which their employees are already strong. The following two sets of phrases uncover and build strengths.

- What part of your job is the most exciting to you?

- Do you have the freedom to perform this part of your job in your own way?

- Does the amount of freedom you have contribute to your motivation and satisfaction with this part of your job?

- What would your perfect job look like?

- What would you suggest we do to make your job more like that?

- Are there some skills you would like to be able to use more?

- What can I do for you to make your job more satisfying and less frustrating?

Perfect Phrases to Build Employee Strengths

- I notice you are very good at _____. Are there some aspects of that skill you would like to develop?
- What would it take to develop that?
- How can I support you in getting even stronger in that skill?
- What do you like to do the most?
- What would you like to learn most?
- You are very strong in the area of _____ and weaker in the area of _____. Mary is exactly opposite, so I'd like you to work together and learn from each other.
- I'd like to give you further training in _____.
- I've got a job that has your name on it because I want to build your skills in the area of _____.

Perfect Phrases for Positive Reinforcement

Positive reinforcement is one of the most valuable things you can provide your employees. Most employees never hear about it when they do something well. Use Perfect Phrases to make certain your employees know. Notice how they all require you to be specific. There should be no surprises at the performance review. You need to offer feedback—both positive and negative—consistently.

- _____ was a very helpful initiative because ....
- This [report] was among the best I've seen because ....
- This work will help us fulfill our mission and vision.
- Commendations and congratulations for ....
- I consider this to be exceptional work because ....
- I am deeply impressed by _____ because ....
- It's a pleasure to work with you because ....
- I can tell you have an excellent sense of _____ because ....
- I see your attention to detail in how you ....
- I respect your broad knowledge of _____.
- I welcome how you consistently go out of your way to ....
- I appreciate your professionalism as shown by ....
- You have been a great asset to the team because ....
- I appreciate the time and thought you put into ....
- I was impressed with how you took care of all the details of ....

- I know it was difficult to …, but you did it!

- It's clear to me from your results that you have been working very hard and I consider your performance very successful.

- I noticed that you made significant changes in this report. Well done! It is more succinct and easier to understand and the conclusions are clear.

- I can see that you've worked hard to streamline this process. Your efforts have cut turnaround time in half. Thank you.

- When you did _____, it made my job easier because ….

- Thank you so much. Sometimes I get so busy I miss the details. I appreciate you keeping me on track.

Perfect Phrases to Uncover and Address Issues and Obstacles

If your employees do not perform up to standards, avoid jumping to judgments about their failures. Sometimes an employee is not succeeding because he or she lacks the skills. Sometimes an employee is not succeeding because he or she does not understand the real issues. Sometimes an employee is not succeeding because there are obstacles in the system. Use these Perfect Phrases to address issues and uncover obstacles.

- I am generally pleased with your performance, especially …. There is one thing I see a need to work on.

- You are expected to …, but what is happening instead is ….

- Have you encountered any obstacles in the workplace that make it difficult for you to do your [job / project] well?

- Are there resources you need that you aren't getting?

- Do you have the resources to do this task?

- Do you understand what is expected of you? Could you elaborate?

- Do you have the skills needed to do these tasks?

- Do you have the proper authority to do these tasks?

- Is there anything in the internal processes that would help?

- If you are lacking the skills or resources, what can I do to help you get what you need?

- What barriers are you experiencing and what can I do now and in the future to help you overcome them?

- Are you getting the cooperation you need?

- Tell me what you think is happening.

- What would you say if I said I think you are an exceptional employee in the wrong position?

- I notice you've been a bit negative and I wonder: are you planning to leave the company?

- Does your environment support the idea that your work is important?

Perfect Phrases to Develop Solutions

Regard yourself and your employees as partners focused on how to solve problems together.

- What do you see as causing the problems you are encountering?

- What would it take for you to meet the deadline?

- What changes do you think we could make at this point to improve the result?

- There is not one best way to solve a problem. What options do you see?

- Let's consider options.

- What obstacles do you see?

- Let me tell you what I think.

- What do you think of this idea?

- Which ideas do you like best?

- Let's weigh the alternatives and decide on the basis of _____.

- Where can you get the information you need?

- What do you think you should do?

- What do you think I should do?

- What do you think we should do?

- May I suggest another way of doing it?

- Give me a picture of how you would guess I see things.

Perfect Phrases to Address Personal Issues

If employees have personal issues, it can affect their performance. Your job is not to care for your employees, but it goes a long way if you show that you care. Use Perfect Phrases to address personal issues and offer your caring, while remaining firm and fair about getting the job done.

- I've noticed a change in your moods. Is there something going on?

- I appreciate your desire to keep your personal feelings private. If there is anything I can do to help, let me know.

- If you ever feel a need to talk, I'm here.

- We do need to discuss your work performance. I don't know why your performance has dropped, and the job needs to get done.

- Your personal life is none of my business. It is affecting your work and that is my business.

- I encourage you to contact our employee assistance program for whatever support you can use. In the meantime, I need to know what I can count on.

Perfect Phrases to Counsel Employees Going Through a Difficult Time

In counseling employees on personal issues, your role is not to act as a therapist, but to empathize, direct the employees to services that can help, and address the workload.

- [Name], I am so sorry about your _____.

- I was sad to hear about _____.

- It has got to be hard dealing with _____.

- I am aware that you are under a lot of pressure.

- Let me know if there is anything I can do to support you.

- If you ever feel a need to talk, I'm here.

- You are not expected to be "up" all the time. Please feel safe to be real.

- I know I can't fix it, but I can listen.

- If we need to adjust your goals for a while, let me know.

- Obviously we need to get the job done, but let's see how we can adapt your requirements to accommodate your needs for a while.

- I encourage you to contact our employee assistance program for whatever support you can use.

- I find support groups to be incredibly helpful. I found one for your situation. Can I tell you about it?

Chapter 10
Perfect Phrases to Handle Employee Performance and Behavior Problems

find that many supervisors and managers avoid problems until they can no longer ignore them. Some wait until the performance review to address issues; others might even choose to ignore problems at the performance review. However, the best time to address a problem is when it begins; this gives the employee an opportunity to correct any missteps immediately, rather than allow bad habits or performance issues to take root.

Perfect Phrases for Real-Time Corrective Verbal Feedback

Corrective feedback is best given at the time of the offense.

- You know the rules regarding [dress / tardiness / safety / etc.]. You are in violation by ....

- [Name], what you just did is unacceptable because ....

- This report was due this morning. I expect it on time in the future.

- Are you aware of the effect of what you just did?

- Company policy states .... You have ....

- What do you believe the rule is? When you ..., it violates policy.

- Are you aware of the rules regarding _____?

- Is there any confusion about what the standards are?

- The standards are .... What you did is .... The impact is ....

- I want you to have the best performance review yet. In order for that to happen, I need for you to ....

- Here is what I [saw / heard / smelled].

- It worries me that you ... because ....

- Perhaps that remark was intended to be innocent. Let me tell you the effect it had on the team.

- When you said _____, I noticed the team members cringe. Let's look at how you can express yourself in a different way in the future.

- You are usually very punctual, but lately this is slipping. What's going on? Perhaps I can help.

- I'm concerned about how your team perceives you with this behavior.

- Are you aware of the impact of your behavior on the [team/customers]?

- Let me tell you how this impacts me.

- We seem to be working at cross-purposes rather than together. What can I do to help change that?

Perfect Phrases to Turn Informal Feedback into Verbal Warnings

The verbal warning is the first step on the disciplinary ladder. If you intend the feedback to serve as a warning for the record, mention it when you give corrective verbal feedback and make a record of what happened and your remarks.

- I am making a note of this discussion.

- I will regard this as the first time we have discussed this.

- This is a verbal warning.

- I intend to document this conversation.

- Please consider this your first verbal warning. As you know from the handbook, you can receive _____ before termination is considered.

Perfect Phrases for Written Warnings and Counseling Sessions

Written warnings are the next step on the disciplinary ladder. Written warnings need to be accompanied by counseling sessions. Be aware that whatever you do in this process can have two audiences—the employee and a potential jury.

PERFECT PHRASES TO ADVISE OF WRITTEN WARNINGS AND COUNSELING SESSIONS

- I want to talk to you about your work progress. Can you meet me in my office at _____?

- I'm worried about your continued [attendance problems / performance / demeanor with the team / etc.]. We've reached the point of a written warning, which I have for you to review. You are entitled to file a response. Can you meet with me at _____?

PERFECT PHRASES FOR A WRITTEN WARNING

- This is a written warning of poor performance and is part of the disciplinary process.

- This constitutes a formal written reprimand to you regarding _____.

- We will meet [date] at [time] to discuss this reprimand.

- You have the right to write a response to this reprimand, which will be attached to the reprimand.

- The purpose of this warning is to make you aware of performance issues and to provide the opportunity for improvement.

- The details of the performance problem are ....

- You [specify behavior], [date and time]. The rule that was violated is _____.

- The effect of this behavior is _____.

- This violation is not unprecedented. On [date] you [specify behavior]. In response, I [specify action taken].

- Your performance is expected to improve in the following ways.

- Failure to improve will result in further disciplinary action up to and including termination.

- If [behavior] happens again, the result will be _____.

- If, after that, [behavior] occurs again, the result will be _____.

- I need you to _____ or I will have to _____.

COUNSELING SESSION TO ACCOMPANY THE WRITTEN WARNING

- This meeting is a step in the disciplinary process.

- The purpose of this meeting is to discuss the problem and focus on how to improve, as well as to inform you of the consequences of continued violation.

- We are having this conversation because I don't want to fire you. I'll fire you only if I have no other choice.

- We have a problem here we need to address. I'll help in any way I can, but it needs to be addressed.

- I need for you to read the reprimand here before we proceed. I'll wait.

- Do you understand the issues?

- Do you really want this job?

- Explain why you broke the rule.

- What questions do you have about the document?

- Have you elected to draft a response?

- If you still wish to draft a written response, please have it to me within two days.

- We'll get a lot out of this meeting if we work together toward solutions.

- You must meet your quota of _____.

- You are expected to ….

- Once this problem is corrected and performance is at acceptable levels for [time period], this action will be removed from your record.

- I'd like to hear your impressions of the warning.

- What do you see as the ideal outcome of this meeting?

- What do you believe you can do to improve your performance?

- You know the policy, but I will explain it to make sure we both understand.

- Your performance is still not at acceptable levels.

- You were given oral warnings and _____.

- The policy says that in order to [protect safety/increase productivity / ensure the flow of communication/etc.] it is required to ….

- It's important for me to enforce policy because ….

- When you _____, it violates policy.
- I need you to _____ or I will have to _____.
- What do you believe the rule is?
- Why do you think the rule is important and necessary?
- What alternative do you think we have?
- How can we accommodate your needs and ours and still obey the rules?
- We want you to be part of the team.
- I need someone to do your job, and I'm hoping it will be you.
- Even though you've received fair warning, I see you still ….
- The rule is designed to _____ and needs to be enforced.
- Here is why I insist we follow the rule.
- Do you understand what is expected of you?
- Why is this behavior continuing?
- First in the discussion, I am interested in facts. Once the facts are established, I'm open to your interpretation.
- What can I do to support you?
- Are there obstacles that prevent you from [complying with the rules / meeting standards / etc.]?
- Please sign here to verify that we had this conversation.
- Let me summarize what you said about the issue.
- Let's schedule a meeting in a month so we can talk about how things are progressing.

Perfect Phrases to Suspend an Employee

- This meeting is for me to inform you that you will be suspended [date] until [date] because [specify behavior].

- This suspension is [with / without] pay.

- To review what was done until now, we have given you verbal notice and a written warning with a counseling session. In those, you were informed that ....

- Normally we have a progressive policy of dealing with performance issues. This behavior is too egregious to allow that. You are suspended pending investigation.

- Your performance plan was to .... Your performance has not improved in the following ways.

- If your performance does not improve after suspension, the next step is _____.

- Your e-mail will be blocked and I need you to return the keys and the company credit card.

- This suspension is intended as an opportunity for you to decide if you really want to work here.

Perfect Phrases to Inform Employees About an Employee on Suspension

- [Name] has been suspended until [date].

- Please do not contact [name] regarding work-related matters. Until further notice, contact [name].

- Out of respect for [name]'s privacy, that is all the information I can provide.

- In order to cover [his / her] responsibilities, we need to pull together.

- I'll need your help to figure out how we can keep things running smoothly.

- [Name] has been suspended until further notice. You may be curious about the circumstances. However, legally and ethically I am not able to disclose any information.

Perfect Phrases to Receive a Complaint

All complaints must be taken seriously to avoid legal trouble. Make it easy for employees to file complaints without fear of reprisal. For routine issues, use Perfect Phrases to Encourage Employees to Resolve Conflict (Chapter 4). For serious issues, use the phrases below.

- I am glad you brought this to my attention.

- I appreciate your coming forward.

- I need to find out what is going on, and anything you can tell me will be helpful.

- Everything you say will be kept confidential.

- If you have any sense of retaliation, please let me know.

- I take your complaint seriously and I will conduct an investigation.

- What happened?

- Who was involved?

- How did you react?

- When and where did this happen?

- Did anyone else witness it?

- Did you speak to anyone else about it?

- Do you know anyone else who might know anything about the incident?

- Do you know of any other similar incidents?

- Are you aware of any evidence relating to your complaint?

- If anything at all comes to mind later, please let me know.

- What that you have told me do you feel needs to be held confidential?

Perfect Phrases to Inform an Employee of a Complaint

- I need to talk with you about something I heard.
- I have received the following complaint about your behavior from [an employee / a customer].
- What happened?
- What is your side of the story?
- Tell me your side of the story.
- What did you do when …?
- How often has this happened?
- When did it first happen?
- Who else was involved?
- How do you feel about me investigating this?
- I will be talking with other people about this. Is there someone you think I should talk with?
- I need to investigate to discover what happened.
- What is your response to the complaint?
- Can you think of a reason why [accuser] would lie?
- Could [employee] who complained have misunderstood your actions and intentions?
- How harmonious has your relationship with [employee who complained] been? (Do not use this if the name of the complaining employee is kept confidential.)
- How would you describe what happened? When? Where?

- Did anyone see it happen?

- Did you tell anyone about the incident?

- Do you know of anyone who might have information about it?

- Do you know about any evidence of the incident?

- I will be interviewing witnesses before concluding. I will keep this confidential and trust you to do the same.

- Because of the severity of the complaint, I will be suspending you [with / without] pay until I have completed my investigation.

- We are conducting an investigation of the complaint and we will file a report once we have completed the investigation.

- You may review the report before we determine what action to take.

- Because of the seriousness of the complaint, we will transfer one of you until we can determine what happened.

Perfect Phrases to Interview Witnesses About a Complaint

When investigating a complaint, use phrases that elicit as much information as possible by asking questions that are open-ended.

- You have been identified as a witness for something that happened.
- I need to talk with you about something you may have seen or heard.
- What did you see or hear?
- When and where did this take place?
- Did you tell anyone about the incident?
- Did [employee who complained] tell you anything about what happened?
- Did [accused employee] tell you anything about the incident?
- Have you witnessed other incidents between [employee who complained] and [accused employee]?
- Have you heard these issues discussed in the workplace? When? By whom?
- Have you ever had problems with [employee who complained] or [accused employee]?
- Did you and [employee who complained / accused employee] discuss [area of work the complaint is about, e.g., invoices, weapons, taking equipment home, etc.]?
- Have you noticed anyone bringing a weapon to work?

- When did you arrive on [date]?
- Did you hear [accused employee] and [employee who complained] talking last week? What did you hear?
- Was [accused employee] at the meeting last week? Did anything unusual happen?
- Did you see an incident between [accused employee] and [employee who complained] last week?
- What have you heard that leads you to that conclusion?
- What do you mean by that conclusion about [accused employee]?
- Why do you believe that?
- Have you discussed this with anyone?
- Who have you discussed this with and what did they say?
- Was anyone else there when that happened?
- Do you have any documentation?
- Did anyone else receive documentation?
- I've heard differently. Do you think the allegations I have heard are invented?
- Why would someone invent them?
- Why do you think others remember it differently?
- I expect this discussion to be kept confidential.

Chapter 11
Perfect Phrases
for Conducting
Performance Reviews

Two misconceptions lead managers to hate giving performance reviews.

One, managers think reviews are about pointing out the negative qualities. (I use the word *review* rather than *evaluation*, because *evaluation* itself implies judgment, while *review* implies revisiting.)

Two, managers often save feedback until the review, so the review comments and/or criticisms are a surprise to employees. That is one reason why the performance review chapter follows an entire chapter of phrases to deal with unacceptable employee behavior. By the time of the review, the employee should know what to expect.

Perfect Phrases to Announce a Performance Review and Advise the Employee to Prepare

- Your performance review is scheduled for [date].

- To prepare, please review your performance goals over the last six months.

- Please review your job description to determine if it is necessary to update it.

- Please reflect on what goals you want to target for the next review period.

- [Date and time] I would like to meet with you for a review. In the meeting, I will go over your performance over the last [time frame]. I would also like you to review my performance as your manager.

Perfect Phrases to Set Expectations and Create Ease

- I know these reviews can be a bit nerve-racking. I get nervous about them too!

- It's not my job to criticize you, but to help you become better at what you do.

- I have arranged to give you my full attention here.

- The purpose of this meeting is to take a look at where you are strong, where you need to improve, where you want to go, and how to get you there.

- To make the most of this time, I'd like you to regard us as partners in this meeting.

- One reason I like reviews is because they give me the opportunity to tell you what I appreciate about you.

- This review gives me the opportunity to help you achieve your goals.

- This review gives me the opportunity to address my concerns and your concerns.

- What do you see as the best outcome for this meeting?

- Your participation is important because ....

Perfect Phrases to Review Performance

- The purpose of this meeting is to review how you've been doing and to help you succeed in the future.

- Let me make sure you are getting my full attention.

- I have your records here.

- Do you think you are meeting your standards and goals?

- This is an opportunity for us to work together to maximize your performance.

- Once we have reviewed your performance, I would like to take a look at creating new goals.

- My goal is to help you succeed.

- Let's review each job standard and goal separately.

- Let's see how your standards and your performance compare.

- Let's see how your goals and your performance compare.

- Where I see your performance to be exceptional is _____.

- You're making a difference by _____.

- I'm impressed by _____.

- Let's compare notes.

- What are you most proud of?

- I try to give consistent, ongoing feedback throughout the year. To help me find out how well I'm doing that, I'd like you to start. What do think you're doing well or excelling in? In what areas have you improved? In what areas do you need to improve?

Perfect Phrases to Address Poor Performance During the Review

- Let's talk about the areas for improvement.

- What do you think of your performance?

- What areas would you like to improve?

- What areas of your performance do you see as weak?

- Do you think you are meeting your standards and goals? If not, why not?

- Given the standards, we need to look at your performance in the area of _____.

- Let's talk about your progress toward _____.

- Here is where I see a need for improvement.

- You are expected to …. Here is what you did:…. The impact on [company/co-workers] of not complying is ….

- If you were in my position, what would you do?

- Let me tell you what I think about _____.

- Does this performance concern you as it does me?

- Are you surprised by this rating?

- Why do you think it is important to bring your performance up to standards?

- How do you believe it affects your co-workers and the company when you do not meet the standards set?

- Is there any confusion about what the standards are?

Perfect Phrases to Develop Goals During the Review

- Let's take a look at setting new goals.

- The best goals are ones on which we collaborate.

- In which areas do you see room to do your job better than the standards call for?

- Although you are meeting job standards in the area of _____, I believe you are capable of more. Do you agree?

- How would it benefit the company for you to target a higher standard in that area?

- What strengths would you like to develop?

- What specifically can you do to improve those skills?

- Where would you like to be in five years?

- What skills do you want to develop immediately?

- I recommend you improve those skills by ….

- How would improving those skills directly enhance your job?

- How will we measure success?

- Here is how I will measure success.

- This goal is set to be achieved by [date].

- Based on last year's results, is this a realistic goal?

Perfect Phrases to Create an Improvement Plan

- Why do you think this is happening?
- How can we work together to bring your performance level up?
- What do you need from me to assist you?
- I believe you can do a great job and I think you may need a little help to make that happen. What would that be?
- I am committed to your success.
- I will partner with you to make this happen.
- I support you 100% and will let others know where I stand.
- How can I support you better?
- What training would help you with the skills you need?
- What coaching do you need from me?
- Am I giving you the resources you need to do your job?
- What are the obstacles in the way of …?
- Give me a complete picture of how you see things.
- Let's consider options.
- Would it help to …?
- May I suggest another way of doing things?
- Let's make a plan.
- Is this a plan you can agree to?
- Is this a solution you can commit to in writing?
- Let's review the effectiveness of this plan when we meet [date].

Chapter 12
Perfect Phrases
for Termination

When the appropriate coaching sessions fail to bring positive results and standards have not been met, or when an employee must be discharged for reasons unrelated to performance, it is difficult to find the words. In the case of a performance-related termination, if you have been doing your job, the employee already knows. Make it as quick and clean as possible and preserve as much of his or her dignity as you can. The conversation will have three parts:

1. Begin with an opening.
2. Explain the situation with a minimum of detail.
3. Close the meeting with a summary of what was discussed and recommend action items if appropriate.

Perfect Phrases to Open a Meeting to Terminate Due to Performance

- I am sorry it has come to this.
- I suspect you have guessed what this meeting is about.
- Please sit down. We have come to a final decision regarding your employment.

Perfect Phrases to Explain the Situation and Terminate Due to Performance

- You were given warnings and your performance is still not at acceptable levels.

- In our prior meetings, we have outlined the standards you must meet to stay on with us and you have not met them.

- You have been told what is expected and been given written warnings, but you have not met those expectations.

- Despite warnings, your performance level has not reached acceptable levels.

- I am forced to terminate your employment.

- Today will be your final day of employment.

- The reasons are as follows ....

- The reasons for this are the ones that we have discussed and that are on file.

- This decision is final. It was based on your inability to rebound from two unsatisfactory performance reviews.

Perfect Phrases to Open a Meeting to Terminate Due to Cutbacks

- It's hard for me to tell you this. I know it's harder to hear it.
- I wish it could be different but ....
- I have bad news for you.
- This is one of the hardest things I have to do.

Perfect Phrases to Explain the Situation and Terminate Due to Cutbacks

- I feel sad to tell you, budget cutbacks have forced the elimination of your position.

- Despite our efforts to avoid having to do this, your job has been eliminated.

- Sometimes reality requires me to let go of people I value. That's what is happening now. I have to terminate your employment, effective immediately.

- I understand that Extraordinary Widgets is looking for people with your qualifications.

- HR has a few leads for other jobs.

- How can I help you pull resources together?

- Personnel will discuss your final pay and collect your office keys.

- Talk to me about your feelings. I can't change the situation, but I can listen and understand.

Perfect Phrases to Reaffirm the Employee and Close the Meeting

- I wish this could have been resolved otherwise.
- I hope you find work that suits you.
- I sincerely wish you good luck in your next position.
- (Shake hands.) Good luck. Please contact [name] if you have any questions on [your noncompete clause / your severance package / handing off work / COBRA].
- I will be happy to provide a reference stating ....

Perfect Phrases to Answer Common Termination Questions

- These are the terms of your termination.

- Your last day is [date].

- Regarding bonuses, you are eligible for _____.

- Regarding accumulated sick leave and vacation time not taken, ...

- Regarding your [pension plan/profit-sharing plan/saving plan], ...

- You will receive your last paycheck on [date].

- You [will / will not] be eligible for unemployment insurance.

- Let's go over what I will say to prospective employers if we receive a release from them signed by you.

- We will notify you any time someone requests information.

- Let's go over what your co-workers and clients will be told about your termination.

- Your medical and insurance benefits [will / will not] continue.

- You are expected to return company property, such as a car, pager, cellular phone, keys, etc., by [date].

- You [can / cannot] say good-bye to everyone before you go.

- The way for you to go to your work area to get your personal things is ....

- You have the [hour / day / week] to gather your belongings.

- We [do / do not] want you to complete pending projects.

- In order to pass on your work to other employees, we ask that you ....

- Whatever questions remain after today can be directed to [name / department].

- I am aware you have pending appointments. We will handle those by ....

Perfect Phrases to Tell Other Employees About a Termination

- [Name] has been terminated effective [date].

- I won't be going into details, in order to protect [his/her] privacy.

- If any of you have concerns about this, we can discuss them privately.

- In order to cover [his/her] responsibilities, we need to work together.

- I'll need your help to figure out how we can keep things running smoothly.

- What suggestions do you have for handling this?

- Let's plan the transition.

- If this creates a particular hardship for any of you, please let me know.

Perfect Phrases for the Exit Interview

If an exit interview is for employment that ended in termination, it is best if conducted by someone other than the one who performed the termination.

■ The purpose of this meeting is to exchange information about your perception of the company and how it treats employees. We also want to tie up loose ends about the termination.

■ How do you feel about how management communicates?

■ Is there anything you believe we should know regarding your experience here?

■ What changes would help employees do their jobs better?

■ What questions remain?

■ Let's review the noncompete agreement.

■ Have you returned all company items?

Chapter 13
Perfect Phrases for Meetings and Announcements

Meetings can be very productive, but many people often consider them time-consuming and not very useful to help them do their jobs. This is because the meetings are not conducted well. The phrases in this chapter can help you make meetings more productive and efficient.

Perfect Phrases to Keep the Meeting on Track

Two of the biggest complaints people have about meetings are that they go on too long and are unproductive. As a manager, you can use Perfect Phrases to keep your meeting on track.

- The purpose of this meeting is to ….
- The agenda covers the following points ….
- [Name] will ensure that we stick to the times allotted for each point.
- Please be brief.
- That's outside the scope of this meeting.
- Let's table that discussion and get back on track.
- That's not why we're here today.
- Let's return to the main focus of today's meeting.
- We'll have to leave that to another time.
- We're beginning to lose sight of the main point.
- Keep to the point, please.
- We better leave that for another meeting.
- What do we need to make a decision?
- Are we ready to make a decision?
- We have 10 minutes. What do we need to do to achieve our goals in that time?
- That's all the time we have today.
- We've run out of time until our next meeting.

Perfect Phrases to Bring up an Issue

- We face a challenge. I am happy to be on a great team that can face and triumph over whatever comes our way. Here is our challenge.

- We have a problem we can't ignore, but we can solve it together. It has come to my attention that ....

- This is the problem .... Now it's our job to turn it around.

- We have an issue we must solve quickly. I'm confident we can resolve it with everyone's thoughts, input, and energy.

- I always appreciate your input on how to face an issue. I have just been informed that ....

- Our recent report raised questions for us. What I want to talk about is ....

Perfect Phrases to Emphasize a Point

Use Perfect Phrases to emphasize the points you want your employees to remember.

- The key point is ....
- What we must recognize is ....
- If you remember one point, remember this: ....
- Listen carefully to what I am about to say.
- Here is the main point.
- This is important.
- You must stay aware that ....
- Here is what matters most about this.
- Here is an interesting fact.
- Everyone, please write this down.
- This next point is critical.

Perfect Phrases to Handle Interruptions

- Excuse me. I wasn't done yet.
- Let me finish. I'm almost done.
- Hear me out, and I will do the same for you.
- Just one more minute and I'll be done.
- Allow me to complete my point.
- I want to hear your point after I have completed mine.
- Hold that thought until I've completed mine.

Perfect Phrases to Elicit Opinions

- What do you think about this proposal?
- Would you like to add anything, [name]?
- Who else has something to contribute?
- Let's find the best way to get this done.
- If you did have an objection to this initiative, what would it be?
- What other comments are there?
- Please tell me what you like about this [plan/procedure /idea/etc.].
- What would make you like this plan more?
- What do you believe could conceivably go wrong with this in the worst possible scenario?
- What do you think of this? You don't have to be right.
- Do you see a better way of doing this?
- What have I overlooked?
- Let's go around the room and ask at least one question each. If we are making any assumptions, I'd like to find out now.
- I want to make sure my instructions are clear. What is your understanding of what I just said?
- What did I leave out?
- What would you like reviewed?
- What do you recommend our first step be?
- Take a moment and summarize our discussion so far.

- What main points stand out in what we said?
- Let's see if I communicated well. What did you hear me say?
- [We/I] can't do this alone. Your input is crucial.
- I need to hear from those of you who have not spoken yet.

Perfect Phrases to Comment on Opinions

- I never thought about it that way before.
- Good point!
- That's one option. What would some others be?
- I get your point.
- I see what you mean.
- Tell me more.
- What else?
- Exactly!
- Very insightful.
- That's [exactly] the way I feel.
- I have to agree with [name].
- Up to a point I agree with you. What I question is ….
- I can see why you see it that way. Have you considered …?
- I'm afraid I don't quite understand what you are getting at.
- Explain to me how that can work.
- I don't see what you mean. Could we have some more details, please?
- I'm listening to you, but I don't understand. What do you mean by …?
- That wasn't what I was looking for, but it is an excellent point.

Perfect Phrases to Correct Information

- Apparently I wasn't clear.
- Let me clarify.
- That's not the point I am making.
- That's not what I meant.
- Let me state it another way.

Perfect Phrases to Focus Decisions

- How do you turn that into action?
- What do [you/we] need to make a decision?
- In order for me to make a decision, I still need ....
- What do you suggest we do about this?
- What do you conclude from that?
- What do you see as the next step?
- If you had to choose a course of action now, what would it be?

Chapter 14
Perfect Phrases That
Empower Employees

Success as a manager comes when your staff members are empowered to do their jobs with autonomy. Use Perfect Phrases that empower to express appreciation, to motivate, and to build confidence. Such phrases give honest praise and engender confidence in employees to take on responsibility and seek to improve their performance.

Perfect Phrases to Express Appreciation

- When you did …, it made my job easier because ….
- I would have missed that had it not been for you.
- Your idea made the difference because ….
- This [report] is exceptional because ….
- I congratulate you for ….
- This work is exceptional because ….
- That was true genius.
- I am impressed by _____ because ….
- I like working with you because ….
- I can tell you are skilled with _____ by the way ….
- I respect your mastery of detail in how you ….
- You worked hard and you did it!
- This report is succinct and easy to understand and it draws very clear conclusions.
- I respect your deep understanding of _____.
- Thank you for consistently going out of your way to ….
- Your _____ professionalism is shown by ….
- The time and thought you put into _____ are quite evident by the way you ….
- You handled the details of _____ beautifully.
- I know it wasn't easy to …, but you did it!
- You are an asset to the team because ….
- You simplified this process in ways I never imagined.

Perfect Phrases to Motivate

- You have the power to make this happen.

- This is not something just anyone could do, but I know you can.

- I can see the skills you'll acquire from this task being valuable for you throughout your career.

- The job you do on this will help us fulfill our mission and vision.

- If you give it your best, I see two outcomes—growth and success.

- Take this on like you can't fail and know I'm here cheering you on.

- I see what you have accomplished last quarter, and I get very excited to imagine what you can do going forward.

- Here is what we are facing, and it's up to us to turn it around. I believe we can.

- I am confident in our ability to overcome this issue and be stronger for having done so.

- If this were easy, everyone would do it. Everyone is not doing it, but we are. I'm proud to be on a team like this.

- I am committed to your success.

- Let's focus on what we want, rather than what we don't want.

- I know we can create the future we want. We just need to agree on what that is.

- Just because it hasn't been done does not mean we can't do it.
- We can find a better way.
- I always appreciate your way of looking at things.
- I'm optimistic about what we will accomplish.
- This company's future is in our hands.

Perfect Phrases to Create Autonomy

- Your input is important to me. How would you solve this?

- I'd like your input before I make my decision.

- I find that most employees are too busy figuring out what I want that they can't figure out what doing a good job means. What I want is for you to figure out what doing a good job means and, if what it means is contrary to your job as it stands, to renegotiate your job.

- Please bring me two or three possible solutions and we will decide this together. It's true I am the boss, but I would not want to implement a solution that doesn't work for you. If you were the boss, what would you suggest?

- What have you tried so far?

- I want you to stretch the boundaries of your job.

- What have you done yourself to eliminate the obstacles?

- How does it appear to you?

- This is a decision you can make without consulting me.

- How would you handle this situation if I weren't available?

- Have you applied all the guidelines yourself before bringing this to me?

- If you *did* know how to handle the situation, what would you do?

- How have you handled this in the past?

- I appreciate how you handled that one on your own.
- In the future I would like you to make your own decisions about ....
- We have a budget of $_____ for _____. I trust you to decide how to apply it.

Chapter 15
Perfect Phrases to
Communicate up the Ladder

A s a manager, the dynamic with your boss changes, as do your responsibilities. This chapter will help you stay in sync with your boss, disagree with your boss, support your staff, keep your boss informed, and present ideas.

Perfect Phrases to Stay in Sync with Your Boss

- Are you satisfied with what I've accomplished so far?
- How would you like for me to update you?
- Did this conversation go the way you hoped it would?
- Boss, it's hard to forecast how I'm doing as we approach my review. Is there anything I can do to meet your requirements?

Perfect Phrases to Disagree with Your Boss

There are times when you feel so strongly about a management decision that you are compelled to speak out. How do you stand up for what you believe without committing career suicide?

Be aware that Perfect Phrases to disagree with your boss carry risk. No matter how tactful you are, you could risk being labeled a troublemaker or worse. As you do in any situation, weigh the pros and cons before you speak. However, also be aware that the more you risk, the more you stand to gain. The strongest managers do what they believe is right, even when there is a risk involved.

- I am uncomfortable with this, based on our mission statement and company values. I'd like to consider other options.

- I'm sure you've already considered mission and vision when this decision was made. It strikes me as inconsistent with our company commitment. How are they integrated?

- I have always been proud to say that my company follows its mission and adheres to its values. I have some serious concerns about what we're doing now. Do you see it as in line with our mission and values?

- I feel strongly about this. I love this company and have always seen it as fair and ethical. I don't think this fits our usual standards.

- I need to resolve something to be able to do this in

good conscience. Is what we're doing in line with our company values and ethics?

- Help me to understand how you reached that conclusion.

- I wonder if we have the same information. My information leads me to a different conclusion.

- I want to give my best here. I can support you better if we can resolve these differences first.

- I want to be clear here. I am sincerely concerned about the direction we're heading.

- I am a team player, I enjoy my job, and I intend to stay here. However, I think we should reconsider this decision because ….

- I have a problem with this. I believe this is a flawed initiative, for reasons I would be happy to outline. What are my options?

- I can see the short-term advantage of this decision. Let me outline the long-term concerns I have.

- I am concerned that if we continue on this path we could all end up in legal trouble.

Perfect Phrases to Warn Your Boss of Developing Problems

Since you have a different relationship with the workforce culture than your boss does, you will know implications of decisions that your boss might be unaware of. You are responsible for letting him or her know.

- There are some things I need to tell you about the culture on the ground here that is affecting the implementation of our strategy.

- I don't want you to be blindsided, so I want to give you a heads-up about trends I see.

- There is a buzz in the grapevine I need to discuss with you.

Perfect Phrases to Refuse the Boss's Request and Focus Priorities

As with disagreeing with the boss, use discretion when refusing a request from the boss. There are legitimate reasons for refusing a request. "I don't want to" is not one of them.

- I understand this is important. I'm working on project X. Is this new project more important?

- Would you like me to set aside what I'm working on now to do this assignment?

- That's a fascinating idea and I'm flattered that you asked me. Let me explain why I don't think I'm the best person for the job.

- Doing this now means I won't get project X done by the deadline. Is that acceptable?

- Ordinarily I would say yes immediately. I'm on vacation next week and don't know that I can complete the project by then. Do you want me to start it anyway?

- I want to say yes. Right now I'm working on three projects for other people. Could you check with them to determine if you still want me to put their work aside for now?

- I would like to do it. I'm pretty swamped right now. Will you help me prioritize my other projects so we can see where this fits?

- With everything I have on my schedule, I can't give this project the attention it deserves. Is there someone else who can take over?

Perfect Phrases to Manage a Difficult Boss

Difficult bosses range from micromanagers, to managers who never offer credit, to bosses whose aggressive tendencies are downright offensive. While it is a risk to challenge a difficult boss, many people find that standing up to a boss is not only possible, but necessary.

PERFECT PHRASES TO MANAGE A DIFFICULT MICROMANAGING BOSS

If your boss seems overly involved in the details of your work, it might indicate a lack of trust or it could be intended as support. Use Perfect Phrases to address the issue.

- I appreciate your attention to detail because I am also very detail-oriented. Are you uncomfortable letting me do this myself?

- When you change small words in my letters, I feel you don't trust me to do my job. How can I win your trust to work with more autonomy?

- I respect your need to be updated on how the project is progressing. If I give you a [daily / weekly / monthly] update, I believe that will give you the information you need and eliminate the need for interruptions throughout the day. Does that make sense to you?

- I am accustomed to working autonomously. While I appreciate your support, I think it would be a better use of time for both of us if we move me toward autonomy in a way that is comfortable for you. Do you have suggestions of how we can do that?

▪ I'm hoping to function more independently of you. If we could schedule check-in meetings, it would help us both be more productive.

PERFECT PHRASES TO MANAGE A DIFFICULT DISTRUSTFUL BOSS

If there is an underlying sense of distrust from your boss, it usually is beneficial to address it directly and resolve it if possible.

▪ I believe part of my job is to help you look good. Do you trust me to do that?

▪ I want you to be confident that I'm doing my job. What can I do to convince you?

▪ We have different management styles. I'd like us to find a way to work better together.

▪ I think we both have the same objective. We just have different ways of going about it. Can we talk about the goals we have in common?

▪ Are you concerned that I'll make mistakes?

▪ Are you concerned that I want your job?

▪ Although my style is different from yours, I believe I can achieve the outcomes you expect of me.

▪ I'd like to define my work more by outcome than by steps. Does that make sense to you?

▪ We seem to be working at cross-purposes rather than together. What can I do to help change that?

PERFECT PHRASES TO MANAGE A DIFFICULT ANGRY BOSS

When your boss is angry, you may choose to deflect it. If he or she is speaking inappropriately, it usually makes sense to address it, particularly if this is something that occurs frequently. Standing up to bullies is often effective.

- I accept responsibility for the error and I will correct it. I can see we need to work out a solution to this situation.

- Boss, I take this very seriously. I will do everything I can to correct the error.

- Let's take a look at the data and see if we can come up with some answers.

- I want to do the best job I can and to have the best relationship with you possible. I am embarrassed when my errors are brought up in public. When I make errors in the future, I'm asking that we discuss it in private.

- I would be very happy to discuss this with you in private.

- I heard you say that [accusation]. Did I hear you correctly?

- I can get your point without [sarcasm / yelling].

- That is a serious allegation. I would like the facts that led you to that conclusion.

- Exactly what do I say or do that leads you to believe that I ...?

- I will be happy to discuss this when we both are calm.

- I am a professional and I expect to be treated as one.

- I react better to requests than criticism. What are you requesting?

- I'd like to arrange a meeting with a third person so we can discuss your perceptions and figure out how we can be comfortable working together.

PERFECT PHRASES FOR GOING ABOVE YOUR BOSS'S HEAD

It is occasionally appropriate to go above your boss's head. Unless you sense danger, protocol dictates that you request permission or at the least inform your boss of your intentions.

- Would you be OK about me bringing this up with your boss?

- If we cannot resolve this ourselves, I intend to take it to your manager. My hope is that we can work it through without that.

- We are at an impasse on this. It is important enough to me that I intend to bring it to the attention of your manager. Do you want to go with me or do you prefer that I do it alone?

- I want to go on record as being in opposition to this decision. I intend to do that by sending a letter to your boss. I am informing you so you will not be blindsided.

- As you know, I am entitled to file a grievance on this issue. I intend to do that.

- I would be happy to discuss this before a review board or mediating organization for unfair employment practices.

Perfect Phrases for Bringing an Idea to Your Boss

Sometimes the challenge in bringing an idea to your boss is getting him or her to consider your idea. Other times the issue is ensuring that he or she doesn't take all the credit for the idea.

- I have an idea that is different from what we have been doing. I'd like you to consider how it might work before you consider the reasons why it wouldn't.

- I have an idea I have run past three of the other managers and they all suggest I bring it to you. When can we meet to discuss it?

- Have you considered …?

- Something you said the other day got me thinking.

- I'd like your opinion about what I did with the concepts you and I discussed last month.

- I have been considering how to increase my department's bottom line, and I have come up with a way to do it.

Perfect Phrases to Break Bad News to the Boss

- I have just made what might be a career-limiting move.

- I have bad news and good news. The good news is that I have a plan of action to deal with the bad news, which is ....

- I need to inform you about an error that I am responsible for and will correct.

- If experience comes from mistakes, I just gained a huge amount of experience.

- I made a miscalculation that I need to tell you about. Please remember my overall performance and years of improved service when I tell you about it.

Perfect Phrases to Support Your Team When Reporting to the Boss

To be effective, you must balance your responsibilities to your team with your responsibility to upper levels and maintain the trust and confidence of both. Some managers are so eager to please upper levels they promise unreasonable outcomes that compromise the people they supervise. Some managers take credit for the ideas of their employees. Some managers are loyal to employees to a point that keeps them from being responsive to the needs of the organization. Your boss and your employees need to know they can count on you. When talking to your boss, use these Perfect Phrases to support your team.

PERFECT PHRASES TO PROTECT YOUR TEAM FROM UNREALISTIC EXPECTATIONS

- Let me check with my staff to see when they can have it done. I will get back with you by noon today with a realistic deadline.

- The team is working very hard to meet the existing standards. It would extend them unrealistically to add this initiative.

- I appreciate the cost-cutting benefit of these new measures. I believed they were unrealistic and put an unreasonable burden on the staff, so I did research to determine standard output of a department like ours. What I found is that we are already at a work level that is higher than average.

- I would rather under-promise and over-deliver. We can have it done by [date].

- I know we have worked miracles for you many times in the past. But we can't continuously work under that kind of pressure. A realistic turnaround time is [time / date].

- If you are committed to this initiative, the team will give it our best. Let me warn you of the risks involved in adding this to our current workload.

PERFECT PHRASES TO PROTECT YOUR TEAM FROM AN INADVISABLE LAYOFF

- Boss, I believe you are considering laying off [name]. Let me tell you why I believe that would be a mistake.

- I appreciate the need to cut costs. I believe laying off [name] would actually add to the cost, because ….

PERFECT PHRASES TO REPRESENT YOUR TEAM WHEN EXPECTATIONS ARE NOT MET

- I know this didn't turn out the way we projected. I have a great team. I will talk to them and find out what happened.

- My team is my responsibility. It is not their failure; it is mine. I will get back to you by the end of the week with what went wrong.

Chapter 16
Tips for Making Your
Perfect Phrases PowerPhrases

No matter how good your Perfect Phrases are, if you don't use them, if you undermine their effectiveness by tone of voice, or if you use them inappropriately, they won't serve you.

Body Language

Has anyone ever told you your face is scary? If so, it is worth the trouble to learn how to hold an expression that does not intimidate. Do you ever smile while you discuss problems or performance issues? If you do, it is worth the trouble to learn how to hold an expression that does not discount the seriousness of your issue.

Body language can cancel out the power of the best Perfect Phrases. Do you cross your arms, put your hands on your hips, or close in on the person you are talking to? You can come across as aggressive and your employees will hear your words as overbearing. Aggression creates a reaction. Do you fidget and look away from the person you are talking to? You can come across as passive, and your employees will hear your words as weak.

Learn to look strong without looking overbearing. Know what your face feels like when your expression is serious, calm, and pleasant. Learn to put your arms at your side and use open gestures when issues are touchy. Learn to look others in the eyes without staring or glaring. Keep your forehead and eyebrows relaxed, move your focus from eyes to brows to mouth to nose, and glance away occasionally. Use your body language to give your Perfect Phrases the impact of PowerPhrases.

Tone of Voice

Does your tone of voice undermine your words? Do you speak in a high or soft voice that people have trouble taking seriously? Do you make statements that sound like you are asking questions? Do you speak in a monotone that is capable of putting a caffeine addict to sleep? If you do, your voice can undermine your words, make people think that you are passive and they don't need to take you seriously.

Do you have sharpness to your tone or an edge to your voice? Do you raise your voice, so people on the other side of the building can discern every word? If you do, your voice can undermine your words and make people think you are aggressive and create a reaction. While you don't want to come across as computer-like, your words have their greatest impact when you speak them with a calm, open resolve. Pretend you are asking someone at the dinner table to pass the butter and your tone of voice will not undermine your words.

Balance of Power

PowerPhrases are as strong as they need to be and no stronger. One manager once told me, "I never start nasty." My philosophy is to never get nasty at all, but to start by assuming cooperation and the best of intentions is a wise policy. If gentler phrases are not effective, graduate to stronger ones until you find the level of strength required to get results.

The 24-Hour Rule

If you find yourself tempted to make a drastic remark or say something that carries a risk, give yourself 24 hours to be certain of your path. You may regret words spoken in anger. It's amazing how different things can look after a 24-hour break.

When Silence Is Golden

Sometimes your goal is best served by silence. Pick your battles and decide when to speak and when not to speak.

If you are truly bothered by something, it is important for you to speak up, but you don't need to speak up about everything that is not to your best liking. Silence is golden in any of these situations:

1. When it doesn't matter that much.
2. When you are too triggered to speak rationally.
3. When your words are unlikely to bring a good result.

When you pick your words, the option of silence may be your best phrase of all.

SpeakStrong, Inc. and the Center for Responsible Communication

SpeakStrong, Inc.

Mission: To increase awareness of the need for truthfulness personally, professionally, and politically among the world community: To provide individuals with the tools and courage to speak their Simple Truth.

The Center for Responsible Communication Mission: To increase awareness of the need for truthfulness personally, professionally, and politically among leaders: To provide leaders with the tools and courage to speak their Simple Truth.

Meryl Runion: Executive Coach Meryl Runion is the President and CEO of SpeakStrong, Inc. and Managing Director of the Center for Responsible Communication. She has helped over 200,000 people speak the simple truth through worldwide seminars, keynotes, workshops, and her weekly e-mail newsletter, *A PowerPhrase a Week*. Her books have sold over 90,000 copies worldwide. Her clients include IBM, Lockheed Martin, and the FBI. Her education includes a B.A. from Vanderbilt University and a master's degree in the science of creative intelligence from Maharishi European Research University.

Books:

How to Use PowerPhrases to Say What You Mean, Mean What You Say, and Get What You Want (New York: McGraw-Hill, 2004).

PowerPhrases! The Perfect Words to Say It Right and Get the Results You Want (Cascade, CO: Power Potentials Publishing, 2002).

Keynotes and Seminars:

And Your Point Is …? How to Use PowerPhrases® to Say What You Mean and Mean What You Say—Without Being Mean When You Say It.

The "SpeakStrong" Supervisor: How to Speak so Employees Listen and Listen so Employees Speak.

Something Needs to Be Said! How to Create an Organizational Culture of Open, Honest Communication.

Enough Is Enough! Getting to the Root and Resolution of Conflict.

Newsletter:

You can sign up for *A PowerPhrase a Week*, the SpeakStrong weekly e-mail newsletter, at www.speakstrong.com.

Contact:

Send inquiries to: info@SpeakStrong.com.

SpeakStrong Vision in Multimedia:

The SpeakStrong vision can be seen in the Internet movie, *A World of Truth*, at: www.speakstrong.com/movie.html.

PowerPhrases in Action:

PowerPhrases can be seen in action in the entertaining *Legend of Mighty Mouth*, at: www.powerpotentials.com/mightymouth.html.

PERFECT PHRASES
for...

MANAGERS

Perfect Phrases for Managers and Supervisors
By Meryl Runion

Perfect Phrases for Setting Performance Goals
By Douglas Max and Robert Bacal

Perfect Phrases for Performance Reviews
By Douglas Max and Robert Bacal

Perfect Phrases for Motivating and Rewarding Employees
By Harriet Diamond and Linda Eve Diamond

Perfect Phrases for Documenting Employee Performance Problems
By Anne Bruce

Perfect Phrases for Business Proposals and Business Plans
By Don Debelak

Perfect Phrases for Customer Service
By Douglas Max and Robert Bacal

Perfect Phrases for Executive Presentations
By Alan M. Perlman

Perfect Phrases for Business Letters
By Ken O'Quinn

Perfect Phrases for the Sales Call
By Bill Brooks

YOUR CAREER

Perfect Phrases for the Perfect Interview
By Carole Martin

Perfect Phrases for Resumes
By Michael Betrus

Perfect Phrases for Negotiating Salary & Job Offers
By Matthew DeLuca and Nanette DeLuca

Perfect Phrases for Cover Letters
By Michael Betrus

Learn more. **McGraw Hill** Do more.